THE SAINT &
THE SKEPTICS

Joan of Arc in the Work of
Mark Twain, Anatole France,
and Bernard Shaw

by William Searle

University of Pittsburgh

Wayne State University Press   Detroit   1976

Library of Congress Cataloging in Publication Data

Searle, William, 1937-
  The saint & the skeptics.

  Includes bibliographical references and index.
  1.   Jeanne d'Arc, Saint, 1412-1431, in fiction, drama, poetry,
etc. I. Title.
PN57.J4S4   809'.933'51   75-26709
ISBN 0-8143-1541-0

Quotations from The Mark Twain Papers at the University of
California at Berkeley, Copyright © 1975 by Thomas G. Chamberlain
and Manufacturers Hanover Trust Co., Trustees under the will of
Clara Clemens Samossoud.

THE SAINT &
THE SKEPTICS

for Kätchen

The figures of poetry and of history can only survive in the thoughts of men by transforming themselves incessantly. The multitude could take no interest in a person of antique times if it did not invest him with its own interests and its own passions.
France, *Vie de Jeanne d'Arc*

CONTENTS

ACKNOWLEDGMENTS

My first debt of gratitude is to Professor James D. Hart, without whose invaluable advice and encouragement this book might never have been written. Several people have read all or part of the work in manuscript and offered helpful suggestions, notably my colleagues, Professors Marcia Landy, Robert L. Gale, and Thomas Philbrick of the University of Pittsburgh. Candace Lisle has also been helpful. Professor Gale in particular was kind enough to loan me the typescript of his forthcoming *Plots and Characters in Mark Twain.*

I have consulted a number of special collections, including the Mark Twain Papers at the University of California at Berkeley, the immense collection of Shaw materials at the Academic Center Library of the University of Texas at Austin, and the Joan of Arc collection in the Special Collections Room of the University of Columbia Library. I wish to thank the staffs of these libraries, especially Mr. Frederick Anderson, editor and curator of the Mark Twain papers. I am particularly grateful to Cardinal John Wright for graciously permitting me to use his extensive collection of Joan of Arc materials. Finally, I wish to thank the Committee on Faculty Grants of the University of Pittsburgh for providing me with funds both to travel to these libraries and to have the original manuscript typed.

Part 3, chapter 4 appeared in *The Shaw Review* 15 (Sept. 1972), with the title: "Shaw's Saint Joan as Protestant." Permission to reprint is here gratefully acknowledged.

PREFACE

This book explores the philosophical questions which have been raised by the canonization of a Christian saint in a non-Christian century. Joan of Arc has been the object of intensive scholarly scrutiny for over a century and a half; yet she remains a highly controversial and even enigmatic figure. One reason for this, I believe, is that few people in this skeptical age are willing to accept her at her own valuation. Take, for example, her view of her "saints." "I believe wholly," she remarked at her trial, "as wholly as I believe the Christian faith and that God has redeemed us from the fires of hell, that God speaks to be by that voice.* Yet Sts. Catherine and Margaret in particular are so obviously legendary that doubt has recently been cast upon their historicity even by the Vatican.

What, then, is the skeptic to make of their appearance to Joan? If it is not evidence of divine inspiration, must it be taken as evidence either of delusion or of insanity? And if so, how can we account for so spectacular an achievement on the part of an illiterate farm girl who had had no military or diplomatic experience? Could a mere madwoman have accomplished what the armies of France had been unable to achieve in nearly a century of conflict?

Nor are these the only difficulties which her career presents to the skeptic: her religious vocation raises questions about motivation and commitment which are made peculiarly poignant for non-believers because she allowed herself to be burned to death under the impression that she was going to heaven. If there is no such place, then what, if any, are the valid motives for such acts of heroic self-sacrifice? And to what extent are moral codes which are falsely supposed to be divine reliable as guides for human conduct?

These questions are explored at length by the three writers whose opinions of Joan of Arc are the subject of this book. Though very different in background, in temperament, and even in religious conviction, Mark Twain (1835-1910), Anatole France (1844-1924), and Bernard Shaw (1856-1950) shared a common hostility to fundamentalist Christianity which is reflected in their common interest in the Maid. Unlike later writers on that subject such as Jean Anouilh and Maxwell Anderson, who are much more exclusively concerned with

*WMT18:147. The remark is historical.

her commitment, these three were greatly preoccupied with the problem of providing rationalizations both for her voices and for her success. Their religious convictions having been formed when the great majority of Christians still believed in the literal truth of the Bible, they had come to regard such etiological questions as crucial. Consequently, they were much more articulate and contentious on the subject of the supernatural than most later skeptical writers have thought necessary.

Each of these three anti-fundamentalists has written, along with many other works on Joan of Arc, one in particular which stands out. They are *Personal Recollections of Joan of Arc* (1895) by Mark Twain; *Vie de Jeanne d'Arc* (1908) by Anatole France; and *Saint Joan* (1924) by Bernard Shaw. None of these works has been the subject of a study of this kind, and the first two have actually received very little attention from scholars. Yet, all three are of consummate interest, if only for the metaphysical points of view which they represent. Indeed, a careful examination of them provides an admirable means of exploring the religious disorientation which has come to characterize our own troubled period.

I have, then, made a study in comparative biography. It centers around four facts in Joan's life: 1) she claimed to have received messages from God; 2) she enjoyed a great deal of military and political success, which she attributed to divine inspiration; 3) being a Roman Catholic, she was presumably a moral absolutist; 4) she was a Christian martyr. An examination of what the three articulate skeptics have to say on these four topics should throw much light on two questions of engrossing interest: To what extent are the legends of the Christian saints and martyrs still viable as myths for the modern world? How much, in our skeptical and iconoclastic age, can be preserved from the wreckage of Christianity?

PART 1

MARK TWAIN & THE MAID

A Faustian View

*After Faust has uttered the curses which free him from
the world, the Chorus of spirits sings:*

> *Woe! Woe!*
> *Thou hast destroyed it,*
> *The beautiful world,*
> *With mighty fist!*
> *It tumbles, it falls in pieces!*
> *A demigod has shattered it!*
>
>   .   .   .   .   .   .
>
> *Mighty*
> *Among the sons of earth,*
> *More splendid*
> *Build it up again,*
> *Build it up in thy bosom!*

*And the paranoiac builds it up again, not more splen-
did, it is true, but at least so that he can once more live in
it. He builds it up by the work of his delusions.*

Freud, *The Schreber Case*

ONE

TWAIN AS FAUST

Oh Thou who Man of baser earth didst make,
And even with Paradise devise the Snake,
For all the Sin wherewith the face of Man
Is blacken'd—Man's forgiveness give—& take!
  Fitzgerald, *The Rubáiyát of Omar Khayyám,*
of Naishápúr from Twain's notebook.

No work of Mark Twain's has perplexed his critics more, or pleased his public less than *Joan of Arc*.[1] In this reverent biography of a Christian saint Twain is apparently flying in the face of his own skeptical creed.[2] Yet he set great store by it. "I like the Joan of Arc best of all my books," he declared in 1900; "& it *is* the best, I know it perfectly well."[3] In a letter dated January 29, 1895, announcing its completion to his friend and benefactor H. H. Rogers, he wrote, "Possibly the book may not sell, but that is nothing—it was written for love."[4]

What accounts for this evident lack of critical judgment on Twain's part? And how can we reconcile his essentially idolatrous "love" for the Maid with his deterministic conviction that "heroisms are not possible. Reduced to a plain statement of their causes they expose the fact that they are not heroic?[5]

Twain's conception of the Maid represents a deliberate reaction against his deterministic views. In "What Is Man?" in what amounts to a direct attack on the Romantic doctrine of inspiration, he concluded that even the man of genius is so completely dependent on his environment that his talent cannot express itself unless it has been nurtured from without.[6] This, he argued only a year later in the essay "Saint Joan of Arc," was not true of the Maid. "When we set about accounting for a Napoleon or a Shakespeare," he observes, ". . . we understand that the measure of his talent will not explain the whole result, nor even the largest part of it; no, it is the atmosphere in which the talent was cradled that explains; it is the training which it received while it grew. . . ." But "Joan of Arc stands alone, by reason of the unfellowed fact that in the things wherein she was great she was so

without shade or suggestion of help from preparatory teaching, practice, environment, or experience."[7]

Thus, in spite of his anti-mystical convictions, Twain accepted the
thesis advanced by his Catholic sources that the career of the Maid was
a "miracle."[8] "Truth is stranger than fiction," he wrote at about this
time, "but it is because Fiction is obliged to stick to possibilities;
Truth isn't."[9] He may well have been thinking of Joan when he made
this remark: he had come to regard her as a transcendent hero in a
world in which, for all that, transcendence and heroism are both
totally impossible.

In my view this incoherent conception reflects the confused
metaphysical stance which Twain adopted in his later years. Though
he often attacked Christianity with savage and blasphemous fury, his
religious views were neither atheist nor Satanist but Faustian. He had
a firm belief in the existence of God; and although, like Satan, he hated
him and despaired of receiving His grace, yet he never ceased to long
for the sort of transcendence which that grace is said to provide.[10]

The crux of the Faust legend is, of course, the bargain with the devil.
But the critic even of Marlowe— unless he is fundamentalist enough to
believe in devils—must interpret that bargain psychologically. And in
fact it is not so much the pact itself as the motive for making it which
serves to define Faust's position. In Marlowe, Faust has already ceased
to be the vulgar magician who had appeared three years before in the
original German Faustbook. He wants much more from Mephistopheles than the ability to perform amusing parlor tricks and play
clever practical jokes. The famous invocation to Helen suggests that
what he really wants is transcendence, and before he turns to magic as
a way of achieving it, he has already despaired of doing so by any but
forbidden means.

But why should he have despaired? Christianity does not discour-
age transcendence. It identifies it as the end of the religious life, and it
even recognizes, in the experience of the mystic, the possibility of
attaining that end while still in an earthly state. What is more, since
Faustus is a student of theology, he must be fully aware of this. If he
turns from the true path it can only be because he is firmly convinced
that it has been closed to him. And that inference is confirmed by his
pessimistic reaction to two other tenets of Christian theology: that all
men sin, and that the wages of sin is death:

> Why then belike we must sinne,
> And so consequently die,

I, we must die an everlasting death,
What doctrine call you this? che sera, sera:
What will be, shall be; Divinitie, adieu.[11]

Underlying Faustus's demonism, then, is a complete moral and metaphysical despair. And in Marlowe as in Goethe Mephistopheles is, psychologically speaking, the voice of that despair.

Moreover, in both cases despair seems to have resulted from an ineradicable feeling of personal guilt and unworthiness. In Goethe's drama, Faust is recalled from suicide when the voices of Easter worshipers remind him of his vanished childhood and thus awaken in him a wild hope of returning to that innocent state.[12] At bottom Faust's longing for transcendence is an expression of his longing for innocence. If he appears to be incapable of achieving it, it is because, like the damned, he is trapped within the vicious circle traced by conviction of sin. Thus, ironically, the very self-contempt which makes transcendence necessary for him appears to place it forever beyond his reach.

A similar pattern can be found in the history of Thomas Mann's "Doctor Faustus," Adrian Leverkuhn, and in that of the most Faustian of Hesse's heroes, Steppenwolf. They too are deeply divided and cruelly self-contemptuous; they too are tormented by a longing for innocence which causes them to idealize childhood; and they too have despaired before reaching a final understanding with Satan. In my view, these striking similarities in such widely differing approaches to the Faust narrative cannot be merely fortuitous; they indicate that that narrative derives its universal appeal from its relation to subconscious sources. In that case we may expect to see it reenacted in a modern setting. For as Freud has pointed out, the theme of the bargain with the Devil is by no means out-of-date. In his "A Neurosis of Demonical Possession in the Seventeenth Century," he writes, "despite the somatic ideology of the era of 'exact' science, the demonological theory of these dark ages has in the long run justified itself. Cases of demoniacal possession correspond to the neuroses of the present day; in order to understand these latter we have once more had recourse to the conception of psychic forces. What in those days were thought to be evil spirits to us are base and evil wishes, the derivatives of impulses which have been rejected and repressed. In one respect only do we not subscribe to the explanation of these phenomena current in mediaeval times; we have abandoned the projection of them into the outer world, attributing their origin instead to the inner life of the patient in whom they manifest themselves."[13]

Like his own Tom Sawyer, Mark Twain was afflicted from boyhood with an unhealthy craving for fabulous riches. That craving was a common one in the period which Twain christened "The Gilded Age". In his "Does the Race of Man Love a Lord?" he explains that since there is no aristocracy in this country, the possession of such riches is the surest means one has here of acquiring "that most precious of all things, another man's envy."[14] And in his case, as Van Wyck Brooks has shrewdly pointed out, this narcissistic hunger for wealth was reinforced by the anxious desire to prove himself which resulted from his childhood insecurity.[15] "Every person can be bought, if you know what his weak spot is," remarks David Shipman in Twain's *The Refuge of the Derelicts.*[16] When the protagonist of "The Five Boons of Life" chooses the boon of wealth, he remarks,

> Now, at last, life will be worth the living. I will spend, squander, dazzle. These mockers and despisers will crawl in the dirt before me, and I will feed my hungry heart with their envy. I will have all luxuries, all joys, all enchantments of the spirit, all contentments of the body that man holds dear. I will buy, buy, buy! deference, respect, esteem, worship—every pinchbeck grace of life the market of a trivial world can furnish forth.[17]

What Twain wanted from money, then, is what Faustus wanted from magic. The same narcissistic wound that inspired his escapist desire for transcendence also inspired his insatiable craving for the envy and adulation of mankind. Hence, in his writings, Twain came to think of the promise of wealth as the principle medium of diabolic temptation.

"In estimating worldly values," he wrote in "Concerning the Jews," "the Jew is not shallow, but deep. With precocious wisdom he found out in the morning of time that some men worship rank, some worship heroes, some worship power, some worship God, and that over these ideals they dispute and cannot unite—but that they all worship money; so he made it the end and aim of his life to get it. The cost to him has been heavy; his success has made the whole human race his enemy—but it has paid, for it has brought him envy, and that is the only thing which men will sell both soul and body to get."[18]

When, in "Sold to Satan," Twain sells his own soul to the Devil, he does so entirely in the hope of becoming fabulously rich.[19] The apparent frivolity of that satirical sketch may well have been intended to conceal a covert confessional purpose, since Twain's appetite for wealth was not to be appeased with the fashioning of idle daydreams and of harmless satirical sketches. It also exerted throughout his life a disastrous influence on his behavior. In 1856, when he was still an unknown and impecunious twenty-year-old "partner" in his brother Orion's unprofitable printing shop in Keokuk, Iowa, he read a travel book which inspired him with the fantasy that there was great wealth to be wrung from the coca which was growing in the Amazon basin. Later he was to describe the episode which resulted from that fantasy as "the turning point of my life." In an article by that name, he explained that just when he stood most in need of ready cash in order to realize this wild scheme, he was able to acquire a fifty-dollar banknote by very unusual means.[20] He claimed to have found it in the wind, but I am almost completely convinced that he actually stole that money.[21]

It was a substantial sum at the time; yet the influence of its theft on Twain's career was greatly disproportionate to the amount involved. The theft not only set in motion a chain of circumstances which, as he claimed, led to his becoming an author but it also endowed him with that tragic sense of experience and that sensitive insight into the workings of the human conscience without which, he also believed, he could never have achieved enduring fame.[22] Twain's Offensive Stranger remarks to the Dervish, "From *every* impulse, whether good or evil, flow two streams; the one carries health, the other carries poison."[23] And in fact the vast advantages which Twain derived from his theft were not to be achieved without cost. For the bargain with the Devil merely serves to reinforce the Faustian self-contempt which has produced it. "A false shame springing from a false pride," broods the protagonist of Twain's unfinished novel *Which Was it?*, "makes me dread poverty and loss of the common herd's consideration, and under this stress my principles turn out to be showy shams, I yield to the first specious temptation that offers. . . ."[24] One surmises that such a theft might have reacted damagingly on the psyche even of a less conscience-ridden man; on Twain's its effect was bound to be disastrous. In childhood he had already presented alarming symptoms of severe depression, including a marked tendency toward self-destruction.[25] In "The Turning Point of My Life" he implies that the episode of the banknote was prepared for by a childhood despair which, resulting from a defective self-image, had led him to attempt suicide when he was only ten years old.[26]

The immediate psychological effect of Twain's crime was that he thought of himself as an irredeemable sinner; he even looked forward in dread to the retribution promised by his Sunday school training.[27]

Within two years of the bank note incident, in a letter to his sister-in-law composed shortly after the fatal injury to his brother Henry, Twain wrote, "Hardened, hopeless—aye, lost—lost—lost and ruined sinner as I am—*I*, even *I*, have humbled myself to the ground and prayed as never man prayed before, that the great God might let this cup pass from me—that he would strike me to the earth, but spare my brother—that he would pour out the fulness of his just wrath upon my wicked head, but have mercy, mercy, mercy upon that unoffending boy."[28] Allison Ensor has discovered here proof that "Sam no longer considered himself a Christian."[29] But this is not the language of skepticism; it is the language of despair.

In the comparative security and prosperity of his middle years, however, Twain was able to keep that despair under control with the aid of two relatively innocuous, if essentially desperate, rationalizations. The first was expressed in the determinism already mentioned, of which the logical implication was that he could not reasonably be reproached for his crime.[30] The second involved a misanthropic projection of his self-contempt upon humanity as a whole—the point being, presumably, that anyone else in his place would have done exactly the same thing.[31]

An episode occurred in the mid-nineties, however, which caused his emotional condition to undergo a drastic change for the worse. It began, appropriately enough, with financial failure. In 1895, while he was still at work on the manuscript of *Joan of Arc*, a typesetting machine which he had counted on to make him a multimillionaire proved to be impractical and had to be abandoned. With the collapse of that speculation, into which he had sunk nearly a quarter of a million dollars, his Faustian dream of fabulous personal wealth ended, ironically, in bankruptcy (MTB, pp. 990-96).

But he was not yet defeated. Leaving his favorite daughter Susy at home in Hartford, he embarked with his family on a round-the-world lecture tour aimed at paying back his creditors and recouping his vanished fortunes. By midsummer of 1896 the tour had been successfully completed. He was in England, awaiting a triumphal return to America, when disaster struck. On August 18 Susy died in Hartford of cerebrospinal meningitis (MTB, pp. 220-26). "It is one of the mysteries of our nature," Twain later remarked, "that a man all unprepared can receive a thunderstroke like that and live."[32]

"Love is forbidden you. . ." Satan remarks to Thomas Mann's Doctor Faustus, whose beloved nephew, Nepomuk Schneidewein, died of the same disease.[33] Like Mann's Leverkuhn, Twain perceived in his loved one's death the hand of a wrathful providence lifted against him. "What a ghastly tragedy it was," he wrote to his friend William Dean Howells that September; "how cruel it was; how exactly & precisely it was planned; & how remorselessly every detail of the dispensation was carried out."[34] Thereafter, turning in rage and pain against God, Twain was to pay for his Faustian bargain in the hell of an intense despair:

> There—that is something which I have noticed before: He never does a kindness. When He seems to do one, it is a trap which He is setting . . . He gives you a wife and children whom you adore, only that through the spectacle of the wanton shames and miseries which He will inflict on them He may tear the palpitating heart out of your breast and slap you in the face with it. Ah yes, you are at peace, my pride, my joy, my solace. He has played the last and highest stake in His sorry game, and is defeated: for, for your sake I will be glad—and am glad. You are out of His reach forever; and I too; He can never hurt me anymore."[35]

Twain's retribution had come at last, and with a vengeance. The terrible idea that God inflicts suffering and death upon children in order to punish their parents was to obsess him for the rest of his life.[36]

In "The Symbols of Despair" Bernard DeVoto succeeds in showing how Twain's anguishing sense of personal guilt led to two impulses which were to color virtually the whole of the serious work of his declining years. The first of these was the Faustian desire to return, by imaginative means, to the relative happiness of boyhood. DeVoto writes, "For we know from his books that boyhood was his golden time and that Hannibal was his lost, immortal idyll, not of boyhood only but of home as well. It meant whatever home means of peace, happiness, fulfillment, and especially of security. In the time of desolation whose symbol he was not yet able to forge, he turned back to the years and the place that meant safety."[37]

As DeVoto realized, however, the world of childhood that Twain presents in his fiction is a violent one. If childhood "meant safety" to Twain, it was not from physical dangers but from moral ones. He seems to have reasoned that children, being relatively free of the moral sense, were on that account immune to serious temptation. "Susy died at the right time," he remarks in his autobiography, "the fortunate time of life, the happy age—twenty-four years. At twenty-four, such a girl has seen the best of life—life as a happy dream. After that age the risks begin, responsibility comes, and with it the cares, the sorrows, and the inevitable tragedy."[38] This remark suggests that

Twain must have dated his own sense of tragic awareness to the advent of adult "responsibility." Doubtless this explains why he never ceased to regard Hannibal as home. The years that he spent there, being free of that moral maturity which had made his own tragedy "inevitable", were free also of the acute feeling of alienation which had evolved out of his adult sense of guilt. "You have spirited me back to a vanished world," he told his childhood friend Jenny Stevens, ". . . in thinking of it, dreaming over it, I have seemed like some banished Adam who is revisiting his half-forgotten Paradise and wondering how the arid outside world could ever have seemed great and fair to him."[39] Like Faust, Twain idealized his childhood as the season of innocence which had occurred before his fall.

This attitude, of course, involves a sentimental distortion of childhood. Faust has already despaired before he makes his bargain with the devil; and Twain's early years were thoroughly guilt-ridden, as he frequently betrays.[40] "In many criminals," Freud remarks, "especially youthful ones, it is possible to detect a very powerful sense of guilt which existed before the crime, and is therefore not its result but its motive. It is as if it was a relief to be able to fasten this unconscious sense of guilt onto something real and immediate."[41]

Twain's fall not only had a profound influence on the locale and subject matter of his fiction but it also exerted a pervasive effect on its philosophy. The second impulse which DeVoto identifies as proceeding from his guilt was the desire to vindicate himself by laying the responsibility for his sins to the charge of God, fate, or natural law. DeVoto, in discussing "What Is Man?" points out that that work is more than a mere reaffirmation of the creed of determinism: it is also "a plea for pardon." "In painting man as enslaved and dominated by inexorable circumstance," he explains, "it argues that the omnipotence of circumstance must answer for what Mark is inwardly afraid he is being held to answer for."[42] "There are many scape-goats for our sins," Twain wrote in his notebook at about this time, "but the most popular is Prov[idence]."[43] And, in a suppressed part of "What Is Man?" he actually argued that God is the author of all sins. "He created a weak Adam when He could have created a strong one, then laid a trap for him which He foreknew he would fall into. Then He punished him when He was solely responsible for Adam's crime Himself. I think He did well to teach people to pray Him not to lead them into temptation. Apparently He knows His own disposition."[44]

The tendencies identified by DeVoto—misanthropic determinism and the need to idealize childhood—profoundly conditioned Twain's attitude toward the Maid's career. To him she was not only a child, and therefore innocent, but a "marvelous child"—the only human being of whom it might be said that "no vestige or suggestion of self-seeking can be found in any word or deed of hers" (WMT 17:xxii). The result of this constitutional selflessness is that she was morally invincible, unlike that Adam for whom God "laid a trap." "What I cannot help wishing," he wrote in "The Turning Point of My Life," "is, that Adam and Eve had been postponed, and Martin Luther and Joan of Arc put in their place—that splendid pair equipped with temperaments not made of butter, but of asbestos. By neither sugary persuasions nor by hellfire could Satan have beguiled *them* to eat the apple" (WIM, p. 464).

In short, in Twain's shoes Joan would not have fallen. "Unconsciously," he declares in his autobiography, "we all have a standard by which we measure other men. . .; we admire them, we envy them, for great qualities which we ourselves lack. Hero worship consists in just that. Our heroes are the men who do things which we recognize, with regret, and sometimes with a secret shame that we cannot do."[45] The knowledge that Twain's reverence for Joan is the reflection of his own feelings of personal guilt and unworthiness enables us not only to explain the unreasoning intensity of that reverence but also to account for the extravagantly high store that he set by the deeply confused and ambivalent book which he wrote—impelled presumably by an obscure desire for atonement—in her honor.

A further insight into these matters can be gained by examining the nature of the concealed psychological conflict which, in my view, justifies tying Twain's career to the Faust legend. In "A Neurosis of Demonical Possession" Freud discovers the source of that ambivalence toward God which I have described as Faustian in the ambivalence toward the father which originates in the Oedipus complex:

> First of all, we know that God is a father-substitute, or more correctly, an exalted father, or yet again, a reproduction of the father as seen and met with in childhood. . . . Later on in life the individual acquired a different, a less exalted impression of him, but the childish image of him was preserved and it united with the inherited memory traces of the primal father to form the idea of God. We know, too, from the inner life of individuals as disclosed in analysis, that the relation to this father was in all probability ambivalent from the outset, or at any rate it soon became so; that is to say, it comprised two sets of emotional impulses, quite opposite in nature, not merely one of fondness and submission but another of hostility and defiance. We hold

that this ambivalence governs the relations of mankind to its
deities. [NDP, p. 104]

In these terms, Faust's behavior may be seen as an attempt to return,
with the aid of religious symbolism, to the unresolved conflicts of his
childhood. In the myth of Prometheus, the Oedipal desire to castrate
the father is projected symbolically in the form of a defiant attempt to
steal God's power. In Faust's case, the same impulse is expressed
through the practice of magic, which devout people have always
regarded with dread as "forbidden." Faust's inability to repent and
atone for this unsanctioned use of supernatural forces may be seen as
the product of his unconscious conviction that the only appropriate
punishment for it is to be castrated in his turn. Indeed, the phallus, as
the source of Oedipal offense against the father, is inevitably the locus
of Oedipal guilt; and it may be that Faust cannot regard any form of
atonement as adequate that does not require him to deny his "man-
hood." Like Satan, he sins from pride.

There is, however, a more revealing way of accounting for Faust's
ambivalence. As Freud suggests in the same paper, the Oedipus
complex normally presents a two-fold character. Just as a small boy's
heterosexual love for his mother makes him want to identify with his
father, so also his homosexual love for his father makes him want to
identify with his mother. Naturally, this last desire is experienced as
castrating, and it is therefore forced into repression. The Austrian
painter Christoph Haitzmann, the subject of Freud's "Neurosis of
Demonical Possession," suffered from just this conflict. "The
feminine attitude to the father," Freud explains, "became repressed as
soon as the boy realized that his rivalry with the woman for the
father's love implies the loss of his own male genital, that is to say,
implies castration. Repudiation of the feminine attitude is therefore a
result of the struggle to avoid castration; it regularly finds its most
emphatic expression in the contrasting fantasy of castrating the father
and turning *him* into a woman" (NDP, p. 109). The dread which Faust
feels for his heavenly Father, then, may also be seen as a projection of
his defensive hostility toward an earthly father whom he dares not
love. In clinical language, he is paranoid about God.

Finally, a further insight into Faustian ambivalence can be obtained
from Freud's observation that, since every neurosis is the result of a
conflict, every symptom must perform a dual function. In order to
resolve that conflict, Freud explains, the same mechanism by which
the psyche secures the repudiation of a forbidden impulse must also

provide that impulse with a disguised gratification.[46] In this case the impulse to take the father as a love object produces, in Freud's words, an "unresolved conflict between a masculine and a feminine attitude (fear of and desire for castration)" (NDP, p. 111). To resolve that conflict, the dread of the father which protects the Oedipal boy from the castrating danger of loving him too much also provides the boy's repressed homosexual libido with the "feminine" gratification of masochism. What makes such gratification "feminine," Freud explains, is the infantile misconception that the sexual activity of the parents consists in acts of aggression on the part of the father against the mother. This "sadistic misunderstanding" produces an intense desire for punishment in the negative-Oedipal male; and it is this desire which, concealed beneath his myriad rationalizations, induces Faust to make his bargain with the devil.[47]

If such neurosis was present in Twain it would explain a number of the most puzzling features in his behavior. It would account, first of all, for his neurotic addiction to self-punishment, and specifically for the morbid gratification that, like Faust, he derived from his despair. It would also account for his Faustian idealization of childhood, since regression to a level of childish dependence is one symbolic means of accepting castration. And it would account for the irrational guilt he felt over Susy's death. As Freud has pointed out, the children of either sex are among the commonest symbolic substitutes for genitalia. Hence, subconsciously, Twain must have wanted Susy to die. He had already confessed to having killed his infant son Langdon through what Freudians would call a "slip" (MTB, p. 456).

If this diagnosis is correct, it is surely significant that Twain identified Joan with his mother, drawing upon his boyhood memories of her to provide important details in his portrait of the martyred girl. [48] "If it is his struggle against accepting castration," writes Freud, "which makes it impossible for the painter to yield to his longing for the father, it becomes entirely comprehensible that he should turn to the image of the mother for help and salvation" (NPD, p. 110). It is also significant that Twain's obsession with the innocence of childhood should have brought him to the virtual worship of a young girl. For to associate innocence with girlhood was, in both cases, to link atonement to castration. It is in Margaret's bedchamber that Faust first perceives an outward manifestation of that peace of mind and purity of heart for which he is anxiously seeking. And in fact his repressed desire to become a girl is what underlies his frustrated longing for "transcendence."

Similarly, Twain's book on the Maid may be regarded as a desperate attempt to share in the longed-for—and dreaded—innocence of girl-hood. Like Margaret, Joan was "deeply religious" [49] and therefore at peace with the father figure whom Twain had offended. Perhaps through his devotion to her he might attain, however vicariously, to that communion from which he felt himself to have been irredeemably barred.

The "magic" by which he achieved this aim was, of course, that of the creative imagination.[50] According to Paine, he made five false starts on Joan's story before he hit upon the idea of telling it from the point of view of Sieur Louis de Conte, her personal page and secretary (MTB, p. 959). Unlike Faust, who relied upon the Witch's Kitchen, his standard method of achieving rejuvenation was to project himself into a youthful persona; and in fact his identification with De Conte is remarkably close.

De Conte is at bottom a superficially medievalized Tom Sawyer. In him the Missouri boy's dreams of intimacy with the great figures of history, of heroic action on the field of battle, and of high adventure in the interests of freedom and justice are finally fulfilled on the great stage of historical romance.[51] And so, naturally, is the most cherished of Tom Sawyer's dreams: that of devoting himself to the protection of a beloved and wrongfully persecuted girl.

This dream was defeated in De Conte's case, it is true, by the irreversible drift of history. In a section of the book which, like the ending of *A Connecticut Yankee*, vividly projects Twain's Faustian sense of personal futility in the face of historical evil, he has the page assume the disguise of a scribe in order to attend Joan's trial, only to look on in impotent silence while the object of his boyish devotion is ruthlessly hounded to her death.[52] The underlying Oedipal fantasy here appears to be that of the small child who is compelled to watch helplessly while his bad father does "horrible things" to his good mother. And in fact it was presumably from the desire to atone to the mother without asking forgiveness of the father that Twain adopted from his Catholic sources an idolatrous version of Joan's career which was wholly out of keeping with his own skeptical views. He ended by representing her, in effect, as a saint in a world without God.

The results were not satisfactory, and it is not surprising that public regard for the work has never justified the extravagant claims which Twain made for it. Torn as he is between the Good Angel of his longing for God and the Evil Angel of his despair, Faust must perforce project into his work the intellectual and moral confusions which result from the division in his soul. Indeed, as we shall see, Twain's Evil Angel led him to betray his conception of Joan as a transcendent figure at virtually every point. Yet even for its contradictions the book is well worth studying; the search for a means of transcendence in a world apparently abandoned by God has become the preeminent spiritual quest of our time. Hence Twain's confusions are identical with those of twentieth-century man.

TWO

JOAN AS VISIONARY PROPHET

Der Gott, der mir in Busen wohnt
Kann tief mein Innerstes erregen;
Der über allen meinen Kräften thront,
Er kann nach aussen nichts bewegen;
Und so ist mir das Dasein eine Last,
Der Tod erwünscht, das Leben mir verhasst.

Goethe, *Faust*

No feature of Twain's text appears more anomalous at first than its insistence on the Maid's powers of clairvoyance, for when he began his research on her he had long been contemptuous of all prophets and fortune-tellers.[1] At that time he had scoffed at some of the claims made for her by her Catholic biographers. Mme. de Chabannes, for example, writes that Charles VII was deeply impressed by the success of one of Joan's predictions. In the margin Twain scrawled "Slush!" and at the top of the page he sneered, "The simple K[ing] was thus convinced that she could read the future."[2]

When he delved more deeply into his sources, however, he evidently allowed them to persuade him that not all of the prophecies which they attributed to Joan could plausibly be rationalized as expressions of Catholic superstition. He was particularly impressed by her claim at the trial that a disaster greater than their defeat at Lagny would befall the English party within seven years. "Now and then, in this world," he makes De Conte remark, "somebody's prophecy turns up correct, but when you come to look into it there is sure to be considerable room for suspicion that the prophecy was made after the fact. But here the matter is different. There in that court Joan's prophecy was set down in the official record at the hour and moment of its utterance, years before the fulfilment, and there you may read it to this day" (WMT 18: 163).

Twain might have reconciled the success of this and other such predictions with his professed Naturalism merely by claiming, as Shaw did, that they were either lucky guesses or shrewd inferences drawn from a direct knowledge of the given situation. In this case, however, De Conte takes pains to rule out the last explanation.[3] And in "Saint Joan of Arc" Twain argues at length that the first would be unreasonable. "There have been many uninspired prophets," he declares, "but she was the only one who ever ventured the daring detail of naming, along with a foretold event, the event's precise nature, the special time-limit within which it would occur, and the place—*and scored fulfilment.*" After giving no less than five examples, including the above, he adds, "Other prophecies of hers came true, both as to the event named and the time-limit prescribed" (WMT 22: 380-81).

Yet if Joan's predictions cannot be rationalized as either informed guesses or lucky ones, how can this extraordinary success be explained? She, of course, was able to answer this question confidently by referring all those predictions to the authority of her saints.[4] For as Twain remarks in "Saint Joan of Arc," "She had a childlike faith in the heavenly origin of her apparitions and her Voices, and not any threat of any form of death was able to frighten it out of her loyal heart" (WMT 22:381). But unfortunately for the coherence of his narrative, Twain could embrace no such "child-like faith." "I do not believe He has ever sent a message to man by anybody," he once wrote, "or delivered one to him by word of mouth, or made Himself visible to mortal eyes at any time or in any place."[5]

Consequently, he was not able to invest in Joan's saints anything which even remotely resembled her own unquestioning confidence. Indeed, he occasionally takes them to task for offering her what he regards as unsound or inadequate advice. Where one Catholic source writes that they failed to confer with her about the women's garments that were forced upon her after her abjuration, he snapped in the margin, "Her saints are merely idiots. They remind her of nothing that is valuable."[6] This view of them is puzzling, however, for if they are "merely idiots" how can we account for the accuracy of their predictions? Granted that they are neither divinely illuminated nor intelligent, where do they get their information?

This ambivalence in Twain's attitude toward the voices, moreover, is reflected in that of his narrator, who is similarly skeptical about the value of their advice. "I was frequently in terror," he remarks in his account of the trial, "to find my mind (which *I* could not control) criticizing the Voices and saying, 'They counsel her to speak boldly—a thing which she would do without any suggestion from *them* or anybody else—but when it comes to telling her any useful thing, such as how these conspirators manage to guess their way so skilfully into her affairs, they are always off attending to some other business'" (WMT 18: 167-68). Yet whatever De Conte's doubts about Joan's saints may have been, they did not prevent his response to St. Michael, whom he claims to have seen in conference with her, from being downright reverential.

His account of this incident is perhaps the most remarkable passage in the entire text. One day, he relates, while wandering in the woods near Domremy, he encountered the Maid seated alone beneath a celebrated beech tree. Intending to surprise her, he slipped into the forest unobserved, and shortly thereafter he perceived what he describes as a white shadow moving across the grass in her direction. Since it was of a whiteness so dazzling that the sight of it brought tears to his eyes, he concluded that he was "in the presence of something not of this world"; this impression was confirmed as it approached, because the surrounding forest began to fill with ecstatic birdsong.

Upon hearing this sound, De Conte continues, the Maid fell into an attitude of prayer:

> The shadow approached Joan slowly; the extremity of it reached her, flowed over her, clothed her in its awful splendor. In that immortal light her face, only humanly beautiful before, became divine; flooded with that transforming glory her mean peasant habit was become like to the raiment of the sun-clothed children of God as we see them thronging the terraces of the Throne in our dreams and imaginings. [WMT 17: 67-69]

What are we to make of this passage? One Catholic critic, Edward G. Rosenberger, has seen in it an "accurately imagined mysticism."[7] And indeed it may well have been intended to permit Twain, through his identification with the narrator, to participate vicariously in the sort of mystical communion from which he was barred by his own anti-religious creed. In spite of that creed he clearly could not banish from his mind the notion that, since man is a corrupt and ineffectual creature in himself, his experience may become meaningful only if it be transfigured by some form of commerce with the divine.[8]

Yet he was usually contemptuous of those who were credulous enough to place faith in angelic apparitions. In an attack on the doctrine of the Virgin Birth which he dictated in 1906, he scoffed at the Virgin of the Annunciation for taking so doubtful a piece of information "at second hand from an entire stranger, an alleged angel, who could have been an angel, perhaps, but also could have been a tax collector."[9] And about St. Michael, in particular, he was quite emphatic. Where one Catholic source claimed that the failure of the English to take Saint-Michael had been owing to the archangel's special protection, he sneered in the margin, "this in 19th century."[10] Surely he cannot have expected his readers to embrace a credulity from which he himself has scornfully recoiled.

The fact is that St. Michael is only the first of a series of angelic strangers who were to appear in Twain's later work, all of whom are endowed with supernatural powers, including powers of prophecy, which are very similar to Joan's. The origin of those powers seems in nearly every case to have been demonic rather than divine. For, as Bernard DeVoto has pointed out, Twain's infatuation for such angels, far from being conventionally pious, was rooted in Romantic escapism. In describing the genesis of the Eseldorf version of *The Mysterious Stranger*, DeVoto remarks that "this was a fruitful time to remember Satan, for Satan is an angel and angels are exempt from loss and pain and all mortal suffering, they are exempt from guilt and conscience and self-condemnation also, and temptation has no meaning for them and they have no moral sense, and neither humiliation nor death nor the suffering of anyone affects them in the least."[11]

Moreover, Twain's preoccupation with this subject resulted less from his interest in Christianity than from his lifelong fascination with dreams and with visionary experiences generally.[12] The "Satan" to whom DeVoto refers is no ordinary angel. As his German name (he calls himself Philip Traum) indicates, Twain actually conceived of him as a sort of pseudo-Christian analogue to those dream divinities who, according to Greek superstition, were gifted with the power to inspire men with prophetic knowledge.[13] Like Faust, what Twain really wanted from Satan was transcendence, for like many men who are afflicted with a neurosis, he experienced the world as a trap. Perhaps because he had remarkably vivid dreams, he had come by the nineties to regard that spontaneous visionary power of which Satan, for him, was the symbol, as the sole conceivable means of escape from the iron web of causality.

Thus, in 1898, while he was still at work on the Eseldorf manuscript, he included in an autobiographical sketch called "My Platonic Sweetheart" a passage which attributes to "the Dream Self" in man an essentially magical creative power. "The artist in us who constructs our dreams," he declares, "is. . .in the instant invention, discrimination, & handling of characters. . .in the faultless drawing & painting of scenery & of human faces and figures; in magic changes of effects; & in general splendor & magnitude of imagination, many hundreds of times the superior of the poor thing in us who architects our waking thoughts." [14] And as if to forestall the objection that the conjuring powers of this "mysterious mental magician" were after all merely illusory, he went on in the same essay to ascribe to dream experiences a reality by no means inferior to waking ones. "In our dreams—I know it!—we do make the journeys we seem to make; we do see the things we seem to see; the people, the horses, the cats, the dogs, the birds, the whales, are real, not chimaeras; they are living spirits, not shadows; and they are immortal and indestructible" (WMT 27: 303-304).

To be sure, Twain's St. Michael, unlike his Satan, is not actually identified as a dream figure. Nor, for that matter, is he represented as demonic. Nevertheless, De Conte's likening of the radiance which emanates from his presence to that of "our dreams and imaginings" is no idle figure of speech. In betraying the dream origin of Twain's angelic stranger, that simile foreshadows his transformation into such later embodiments of "the Dream Self" as no. 44, who appears in the "Printshop" version of *The Mysterious Stranger,* and as Superintendent of Dreams, who figures in the unfinished fantasy "The Great Dark." Indeed, one of no. 44's own apparitions is described in language which is strikingly similar to that used by De Conte in his description of Saint Michael. [15] Yet both he and the Superintendent of Dreams are distinctly Mephistophelian. Not only are they endowed with the love of savage laughter and the corresponding mania for playing practical jokes which the popular mind has always associated with the demonic but they are also gifted with essentially magical powers of creation and transformation. Like Satan, "the Dream Self" is both immortal and immaterial, and can therefore set at naught all merely physical limitations. [16]

However great may be his command over the spirit world, the power of this mental Mephistopheles obviously does not extend to the realm of material reality, and for that reason Twain's Faustian attempt to achieve through him some form of permanent relief from the pain of such reality was clearly doomed from the start. In a poignant notebook entry dated a little over a year after the death of his wife, he wrote, "At 8 A.M. a beautiful dream and vividly real. Livy. Conversation of two or three minutes. I said several times 'then it was only a dream, only a dream.' She did not seem to understand what I meant."[17]

Thus the escapist notion that dreams are a reality proved to be ineffective as an anodyne, and the antithetical nihilist idea that reality is a dream—which was surely the most desperate of Twain's Faustian attempts to rationalize his guilt—succeeded no better. As he had indicated a year earlier in the manuscript of *Which Was It?*, the daily nightmare of guilt and remorse from which one appears to awaken only while one is asleep returns inexorably with each reviving dawn. The guilt-ridden protagonist of that work, waking from a troubled sleep "with a vague sense of having passed through a desolating dream, which has melted away and gone from him like a cloud," has a sudden revulsion in which he experiences "that ghastly sinking at the heart which comes when we realize that the horror which seemed a dream was not a dream but reality." "It is an overwhelming moment," Twain explains, "the last perfection of human misery, it is death in life; we do not know how to take up our burden again, the world is empty, the zest of existence is gone" (WWD, p. 242). And in the manuscript of "What Is Man?", in an attack on the cruelty of God which recalls the death of his favorite daughter Susy, Twain indicates that he was only too familiar with that "last perfection of human misery." A "Young Man" remarks, "He gives us many, many happinesses; and He never gives us pain except by our own fault or for our own good," Twain's "Old Man" replies:

> The happinesses seem to be traps and to have no other intent. He beguiles us into welding our heart to another heart—the heart of a child, perhaps—the years go by, and when at last that companionship has become utterly precious, utterly indispensable, He tears the hearts apart, He kills the child. Sleep comes upon us and in it we forget our disaster. In the morning we wake; we are confused; we seem to have had a bad dream. Then suddenly full consciousness comes, and we know! All the happiness that could be crowded into a lifetime could not compensate the bitterness of that one moment. And thenceforth the rest of our years are merely a burden. This is to discipline us? Is that your idea?[18]

In short, Twain could find no relief from his pain in any form of Romantic confusion of illusion with reality. Even his *Joan of Arc* appears to confirm this fact; although Joan did undoubtedly derive consolation for her martyrdom from her voices, De Conte apparently could not. His only comment on that event is, "Yes, she was gone from us: JOAN OF ARC! What little words they are, to tell of a rich world made empty and poor!" (WMT 17: 282). By 1898 the pain of Joan's loss had apparently merged in Twain's mind with that of Susy's. In that year, recalling this passage in a notebook sketch for a literary tribute to his daughter, he wrote, "The last ms. of mine that ever I read to her was four-fifths of the last chapter of Joan—and the last words of that which I read were 'How rich was the world etc.' And to me these words have a personal meaning now" (MTNB, p. 318).

Nor was this pessimistic view of the matter confined to *Joan of Arc*. Indeed, all those fantasies in which Twain attempted, toward the end of his life, to project his long-standing interest in the magical power of dreams into a coherent vision of human experience tended to confirm the Faustian moral that the imagination alone cannot save us from despair. The very fact that none of the "Mysterious Stranger" manuscripts was finished, not to mention the aimlessness with which all the manuscripts were written, suggests the Marlovian insight that magic and the visionary are both without meaning when divorced from a sense of religious purpose. This impression is confirmed by that pessimistic passage in which Twain, in what seems to have been a sudden burst of inspiration, anticipated what he called "The Conclusion of the Book."

In that conclusion no. 44, the last of the dream-angels around which those works focus, confides in the Tom Sawyer-like protagonist whom he has befriended the secret of his own unreality. "I myself have no existence," he declares, "I am but a dream—your dream, creature of your imagination. In a moment you will have realized this, then you will banish me from your visions and I shall dissolve into the nothingness out of which you made me. . ." And after a bitter, Faustian denunciation of God, Man, and the World, he ends by pronouncing that nihilistic creed which Twain evidently intended to be taken as the moral of the work:

> It is true, that which I have revealed to you: there is no God, no universe, no human race, no earthly life, no heaven, no hell. It is all a Dream, a grotesque and foolish dream. Nothing exists but You. And You are but a *Thought*–a vagrant Thought, a useless Thought, a homeless Thought, wandering forlorn among the empty eternities![19]

Thus a creative enterprise which seems to have sprung from a firm confidence in the reality of dreams ended with a despairing affirmation of the dreamlike and therefore illusory character of all human experience.

THREE

JOAN AS WOMAN OF THE PEOPLE

*The way to innocence, to the uncreated and to God
leads on, not back, not back to the wolf or to the child, but
ever further into sin, ever deeper into human life.*

Hesse, *Steppenwolf*

Apart from the voices, much that has been recorded of Joan may reasonably puzzle the skeptical historian, and Twain's Catholic sources naturally took pains to point that fact out. The Irish biographer John O'Hagan, for example, urging Joan's canonization in his *Joan of Arc,* scoffs at those who would count "upon natural principles of enthusiasm and delusion" for what he calls "all this wonder—this undeniable history of an unlettered child, who, in her obscure hamlet, not only declares herself commissioned from on high to deliver her country, but from the beginning details with luminous precision the means by which that deliverance was to be effected.[1] Twain, who scored this passage without comment, was quick to concede the "Wonder" of the Maid's history. Indeed, in "Saint Joan of Arc" he calls her "the Wonder of the Ages," citing "her origin, her early circumstances, her sex, and that she did all the things upon which her renown rests while she was still a young girl" (WMT 22: 376). But unlike O'Hagan, he refused to conclude from this position that "the Arm which had of old sent forth a shepherd boy for the salvation of Israel was not shortened, and once more raised up the weak ones of this world to confound the strong." In keeping with his Faustian rejection of Providence, he held that there is "no instance on record where He has shown any interest at all in any human squabble, nor whether the good cause won out or lost."[2] Accordingly, he repudiated out of hand the notion that faith is a more potent instrument than personal talent. Another of his Catholic sources attempted to account for Joan's popularity with the common people by explaining that "it is the privilege of poverty to perceive God more readily in the person of his emissaries, for whence he chooses his instruments he also derives his witnesses." Twain snorted in response, "It seems so

great & wonderful that he should choose his instruments by preference among the dull & the ignorant that I marvel he does not choose
cats—His glory would be the greater & the argument is the same."[3]

By the same token, Twain rejected O'Hagan's contention that Joan
ought to be made a saint; he simply felt no reverence for that holy
estate. "Joan never asked for saintship. . ." he insists in a footnote to
the novel (WMT 18: 51). And in a passage in the manuscript he makes
De Conte complain of the voices that, being saints, they had "the
saint's natural incapacity for business." "Whatever a saint is," the
page explains, "he is not clever. There are acres of history to prove
it. . . . The Voices meant Joan nothing but good, and I am sure they
did the very best they could with their equipment; but I also feel sure
that if they had let her alone her matters would sometimes have gone
much better."[4]

Twain, like Shaw, attributed Joan's success not to the intervention
of Providence but to her "natural capacity for business." "*I* think these
vast powers and capacities were born in her," he makes De Conte
explain, "and that she applied them by an intuition which could not
err" (WMT 17: 304). But Shaw's Vitalism enabled him to discover in
such "vast powers and capacities" a plausible explanation for her
achievement. Twain, in keeping with his conception of her as a
transcendent figure, insisted that not even they could account for it.
For as we have seen, he held that native talent can find expression only
when it has been carefully nurtured by a favorable environment; and
Joan's environment, in his view, was anything but favorable. "We can
comprehend," he declares in "Saint Joan of Arc," "how she could be
born with these great qualities, but we cannot comprehend how they
became immediately usable and effective without the developing
forces of a sympathetic atmosphere and the training which comes of
teaching. . ." (WMT 22: 378).

But why, it may be asked, should Twain have chosen for the subject
of a historical novel a figure whose relation to her environment he
admitted he could neither explain nor understand? The answer seems
to be that in *Joan of Arc*, as in *A Connecticut Yankee*, he was projecting
his Faustian desire for transcendence into history—with the result
that his deepest personal problems, including specifically his escapist
desire for some form of supernatural grace, appeared to have rele-
vance within the sphere of society. He seems to have reasoned that if a
mechanical causality has imprisoned "the damned human race"
within its history, then its salvation can come only through the intru-

sion into that history of essentially uncanny forces appearing from
without.

At all events, Twain ardently desired to believe that Joan's powers
were really uncanny.[5] In some places he even hints that such a belief
would not be inconsistent with his own Faustian rejection of Providence. *"And whether she comes of God or no,"* he makes one of her
supporters declare, "there is that in her heart that raises her above
men—high above all men who breathe in France today—for in her is
that mysterious something that puts heart into soldiers, and turns
mobs of cowards into armies of fighters that forget what fear is when
they are in that presence. . . that is the spirit that can save France, and
that alone, *come it whence it may!"* (WMT 17: 129; my emphases).

What was that "mysterious something"? And what relation did it
bear to the "riddle" of Joan's genius? If her "vast powers and
capacities" were not developed by her environment, must we assume
that, like those of Mann's "Doctor Faustus," they had received some
unnatural heightening? In the light of Twain's rejection of Providence
that inference seems reasonable enough. But Twain refused to draw it.
Indeed—while making it clear that his motives for doing so were
realist rather than religious—he even scoffed at those of her followers
who were troubled by such questions. He bristled with contempt, for
instance, for the tribunal which the Dauphin established at Poitiers to
inquire into the Maid's credentials as a messenger of God. "Instead of
setting a military commission" De Conte complains, "to find out if
this valorous little soldier could win victories, they set a company of
holy hair-splitters and phrase-mongers to work to find out if the
soldier was sound in her piety and had no doctrinal leaks" (WMT 17:
160). It seems not even to have occurred to the page at this point that a
seventeen-year-old girl without military experience could hardly have
proven an ability to "win victories" by purely natural means.

Thus the "riddle" of Joan's "genius" remains unsolved in Twain's
text. And those of her exploits which appear to be supernatural in
character—such as her telepathic discovery of a sword beneath the
altar of Our Lady of Fierbois and her clairvoyant penetration of the
disguise of the Dauphin in his court at Chinon—are reduced in the
novelist's hands to vulgar magical tricks. Their only significant historical function appears to be that of arousing martial enthusiasm in a
superstitious populace. In this respect, as in many others, *Joan of Arc*
bears a striking resemblance to *A Connecticut Yankee in King Arthur's
Court*–a work which Twain had finished in 1889 only a few weeks

before. In Joan's case as in the Yankee's it is public superstition rather than private charisma which appears as the ultimate motive force behind the elaboration of human destiny. And as a result, Twain's position that she could succeed only by transcending her environment is very seriously compromised.

At one point, for instance, he undermines his claim that she was endowed with "a mysterious something that puts heart into soldiers" by attributing the martial enthusiasm she aroused to what he calls a "superstitious reverence" (WMT 17: 194-95). And going even farther in her case than in that of the Yankee, he actually came to attribute a major role in her achievement to the presence of "superstitious reverence" in herself. Where one of his Catholic sources praises her for the frequency with which she attended confession, he wrote, "Think of this heroic soul in such company—& yet nothing but this base superstition could lift her to that fearless height."[6]

What is more, he represents Joan as deriving very significant support from just such "base superstition." Unlike the Yankee, who denounces the doctrine of the divine right of kings as an "invention" of the Church to secure the subjection of the common people, she believes devoutly in the sacramental efficacy of coronation. So she arranges the Dauphin's crowning in person, taking particular care to see that the ceremony follow the prescribed ritual. "In a word," the page explains, "an uncrowned king is a *doubtful* king; but if God appoint him and His servant the Bishop anoint him, the doubt is annihilated; the priest and the parish are his loyal subjects straightway, and while he lives they will recognize no king but him." The Maid's acceptance of this view, he continues, "shows you as in a mirror—for Joan was a mirror in which the lowly hosts of France were clearly reflected—that to all that vast underlying force called 'the people,' he was no King but only Dauphin before his crowning, and was indisputably and irrevocably King *after* it!" (WMT 18: 29).

Thus, failing to bring his perception of Joan's career into line with his Faustian conception of her as a transcendent figure, Twain ended by representing her achievement as due in large part to her direct involvement in medieval tradition. In this respect she forms a particularly instructive contrast to the Yankee, whose relation to that tradition remains always that of an outsider. Thus he never allows himself to become an object of "superstitious reverence," his own democratic "training" having rendered him contemptuous of all reverence that is not rational. Unlike Joan, who "was of the people and knew the people" (WMT 17: 28), he refuses to accept knighthood, remarking, "I couldn't have enjoyed such a thing with my notions. . ." (WMT 14: 63-66). Yet his experience actually indicates that men can be governed effectively only by imposing on their credulity; and in fact his failure to become assimilated into the structure of medieval society proves ultimately to be disastrous for him. It ensures his alienation from the very people whom he is striving to reform.

Apparently the moral is the same in both cases: humanity is too superstitious to be governed by rational appeals to its interests; hence the Faustian project of transforming it through a superhuman transcendence of its prejudices is doomed form the start. Constructive reform in any society must grow naturally out of its own institutions, for unless such reform is the expression of a general increase in public enlightenment, it can be neither effective nor enduring.

This observation goes to the heart of the Faust legend. If we translate it from the social sphere into the personal, it apparently reflects an awareness of the futility which underlies Faust's desperate effort to escape from his despair by supernatural means. In Goethe, for instance, one of the first things which Faust learns after making his pact with Mephistopheles is that he cannot get rid of his guilt by magic; the witch's brew which gives him physical rejuvenation leaves him as old as ever in spirit and hence as remote as ever from the childlike innocence which he is actually seeking. The lesson to be learned from this failure goes beyond the trite observation that innocence, once lost, can never be regained. It lies rather in the larger insight that since in the realm of the spirit there can be no short cuts, one cannot constructively alter one's nature by any non-natural means. The failure to recognize this fact was Faust's most obvious mistake. And, as if in confirmation of the medieval view that the vicissitudes of the microcosm are reflected in those of the macrocosm, such failure also accounts for the disastrous collapse of the Yankee's England. Like Faust, what Arthur's kingdom needed was neither transcendent power nor transcendent knowledge, but the sort of strength and of wisdom which can come only from an entirely natural process of spiritual growth.

This insight takes on a special significance in an age in which science has proliferated power and knowledge without apparent regard for either strength or wisdom. Some critics have even discerned in the fact that Joan succeeds where the Yankee fails an indication that by the early nineties Twain and many of his contemporaries had begun to react against modern technology in favor of the faith of the Middle Ages. Twain's friend William Dean Howells wondered, in discussing *Joan of Arc*, what to say to its heroine's career "in the last year of this incredulous old century, nodding to its close." Pointing out that "it was she who recreated France, and changed her from a province of England to the great monarchy she became," he asks, "could a dream, an illusion, a superstition, do this? What then are dreams and illusions and superstitions that our wisdom should be so eager to get rid of them?"

Howells then complains, in a manner reminiscent of Henry Adams, that "the force that could move mountains is pretty much gone out of the world," and that the substitution of electricity for it has not proven satisfactory. He concludes with a rueful reference to the newly discovered use of electricity to "exanimate people" which brings to mind the mass execution at the end of *A Connecticut Yankee*.[7] Modern man, he implies, has abandoned faith in God in return for mechanical power over nature, only to learn that he, like Faust, has made a devil's bargain.

Yet the *Yankee*, with its Faustian contempt for Catholic tradition and the medieval past, was not intended to vindicate the faith of the Middle Ages at the expense of an "incredulous old century."[8] And *Joan of Arc* too fails, when closely examined, to bear out the contention that religious faith represents a less dangerously insidious form of power than technological knowledge. For if Joan is like the Yankee in having come to prominence through the influence of Catholic superstition, she is like him also in having been defeated by it. Take, for instance, her belief in the sacrament of confession. Whatever its efficacy may have been in lifting her to "that fearless height," that belief, according to Twain, became a powerful weapon against her in the hands of her enemies. By eavesdropping at the confessional, Cauchon was able to exploit it as a means of prying into her secrets and thus ultimately was able to entrap her (WMT 18: 167). Two other pious illusions were similarly instrumental in bringing about her destruction: the belief in the sacramental efficacy of coronation, which inspired in the English the desire to discredit her; and the belief in the existence of supernatural personages, which suggested the most effective means of accomplishing that purpose. "Of course no one doubted," De Conte explains in discussing the conduct of the trial, "that she had seen supernatural beings and been spoken to and advised by them. . . . It would have been foolish to doubt these things, for we all know that the air is full of devils and angels that are visible to traffickers in magic on the one hand and to the stainlessly holy on the other; but what many and perhaps most did doubt was, that Joan's visions, Voices, and miracles came from God. It was hoped that in time they could be proven to have been of satanic origin" (WMT 18: 158).

Thus, ironically, Joan was destroyed by the very delusions through which she had sought to bring deliverance. This suggests still another Faustian moral to be drawn from her career: there is in fact no real deliverance to be found in such delusions. It may be true, as Howells implies, that modern advances in technology have failed to bring about corresponding advances in moral and spiritual enlightenment; but the hope of redeeming that failure through a return to the superstitions of the Christian Middle Ages is clearly a misguided one even from the Christian point of view. It merely projects into the sphere of culture the same morbid desire to escape from what one is that had started Faust on his wrong-headed quest for rejuvenation. And since the law of life is the law of growth, in the social sphere as in the personal, no good can be expected from any such willful regression to an outmoded condition of mind. On the contrary, any attempt to make man's salvation depend upon "dreams and illusions and superstitions" must end by defeating its own purposes. For, as Everyman learns, the only reliable guide to salvation is knowledge. Did not Jesus declare, "And ye shall know the truth, and the Truth shall make you free"?[9]

FOUR

JOAN AS WARRIOR PATRIOT

Wohl! Ein Wunder ist's gewesen!
Lässt mich heute nicht in Ruh;
Denn es ging das ganze Wesen
Nicht mit rechten Dingen zu.
        Goethe, *Faust*

Just as Twain's Faustian alienation from God conditioned his attitude toward Joan's success, it also profoundly influenced his conception of her values. His desire to believe that offenses against the moral law are not therefore offenses against God led him to reject the idea that moral law has been divinely decreed and that conformity to its dictates must therefore come before any other commitment. "I believe," he wrote at some time in the eighties, "that the world's moral laws are the outcome of the world's experience. It needed no God to come down out of heaven to tell men that murder and theft and the other immoralities were bad, both for the individual who commits them and for society which suffers from them." In the next paragraph he added, "If I break all these moral laws, I cannot see how I injure God by it, for he is beyond the reach of injury from me. . . . Consequently I do not see why I should either be punished or rewarded hereafter for the deeds I do here" (WIM, p. 57).

Thus Twain's Faustian stance led him to adopt what amounts to a secularist ethic. In keeping with it, he does actually represent the Maid, in an invented episode, as violating the ninth commandment to fulfill an immediate earthly objective. Joan, on her way from Vaucouleurs to Chinon, gets her little band of followers through the enemy lines by deceiving a Burgundian captain. The ruse preys on her conscience at first, but she is assured "that in the perils and necessities of war deceptions which help one's own cause and hurt the enemy's were always permissible." This classic rationalization fails to satisfy her, however; in the end one of her companions is impelled to remind her that, when asking for permission to leave Domremy, she had actually told her parents only that she was going to visit her uncle, Durand Laxart:

> "I see now," said Joan, sorrowfully, "I told no lie, yet I deceived. I had tried all other ways first, but I could not get away, and I *had* to get away. My mission required it. I did wrong, I think, and am to blame."
>
> She was silent a moment, turning the matter over in her mind, then she added, with quiet decision, "But the thing itself was right, and I would do it again." [WMT 17: 117]

On the surface, at least, this position appears to be confused. But De Conte, in one of the few passages which Twain reworked in the manuscript, is at pains to deny that there is any real contradiction in Joan's thinking here. "If we had known her as well as she knew herself," he declares, "and as her later history revealed her to us, we should have perceived that she had a clear meaning there, and that her position was not identical with ours, as we were supposing, but occupied a higher plane. She would sacrifice herself—and her *best* self; that is, her truthfulness—to save her cause; but only that; she would not buy her *life* at that cost; whereas our war-ethics permitted the purchase of our lives, or any mere military advantage, small or great, by deception."[1]

In Twain's view, then, violations of moral principle are justifiable provided they be performed unselfishly and in furtherance of a worthy cause.[2] But, as he defines it here, this position is problematic. Obviously, there can be no clear distinction between "mere military advantage" and the interests of a cause that can be accomplished only by military means. Moreover, in the nature of things "the perils and necessities of war" must often require infringements of "the world's moral laws" which are far more serious than mere fib-telling. One of the charges which was actually brought against Joan at her trial was that "she incites men to war, and to the spilling of human blood. . ." (WMT 18: 201). Twain in fact represents her as retaining two homicidal fanatics on her own personal staff.[3]

To be sure, Joan was not troubled by any scruples on the score of her soldiership. "I was not ever fond of wounds and suffering," she remarks at one point, "nor fitted by my nature to inflict them. . . . But by His angels God laid His great commands upon me, and could I disobey?" (WMT 18: 57-58). Not sharing these pious sentiments, however, Twain was compelled to work out her vindication in purely secular terms. And considering that what was at stake was nothing less than his conception of her as a transcendently innocent heroine, it is unfortunate that he did not enjoy more success in so doing.

Part of the problem lay in his inveterate Francophobia. His admiration for Joan as the savior of France was qualified from the outset by a deep-seated conviction that France was hardly worth saving. Hence, while he permits his French page to speak of her as "the spirit of France made flesh" (WMT 17: 225), he often scoffs at similar claims made for her by her Gallic apologists. One French bishop refers ruefully to the "touching spectacle" of the French court's attempt to erect a stake to the "liberatress of their native land." Twain's cryptic comment, in bad French, is "car se sont des Françaises."[4] And he described as "stupid" Michelet's claim that only a Frenchwoman would have been uninhibited enough to undertake the journey from Vaucouleurs to Chinon in the presence of men.[5]

If, then, Joan was indeed "the spirit of France made flesh," it was presumably not by virtue of any moral characteristic which she shared in common with her countrymen. Twain could no more identify with her love of country than he could with her love of God. Yet, being an ardent democratic individualist, he had persistently refused to condone irrational nationalism. In the essay "Concerning Copyright," the president thus addresses the nation's authors: "You have diligently and faithfully taught and trained the children of the Republic in lofty political and social ideals, and in that love of country and reverence for the flag which is Patriotism—and without you this would be a Russia to-day, with not an intelligent patriot in it. . . ."[6] If an "intelligent patriot" is one who loves his country because it embodies "lofty political and social ideals," then Joan presumably was not one. Twain believed, as this reference to Russia indicates, that such a country must necessarily be an enlightened republic; and Joan, as De Conte concedes, was a devout monarchist. "The King is my Lord," she declares at one point; "I am his servant" (WMT 18: 59).

This remark is historical; yet its presence in Twain's text nevertheless raises the question whether Twain's Faustian misanthropy had come, by the mid-nineties, to undermine his faith in democracy. Here again comparison between Joan and the Yankee is instructive; Hank Morgan's problem is precisely that of arousing "lofty political and social ideals" in a medieval society whose people have been demoralized by centuries of aristocratic misrule. His program, moreover, for dealing with that problem is based on a classic democratic doctrine: since man's nature is basically sound, the evil in him must be regarded as the result of faulty training. Hence, he reasons, all that need be done to change him for the better is to change his training for the better. But his claim that "where every man in a state has a vote, brutal laws are impossible" (WMT 14: 237) rings hollow in the light of the failure of his democratic experiment. His grandiose dreams of human improvement terminate ironically in a vision of the unmitigated moral horror of war.

That vision carried over into *Joan of Arc*:

> We struck the bonds from the prisoner and told him he was free. His crawling humbleness changed to frantic joy in a moment, and his ghastly fear to a childish rage. He flew at that dead corpse and kicked it, crammed mud into its mouth, laughing, jeering, cursing, and volleying forth indecencies and bestialities like a drunken fiend. It was a thing to be expected: soldiering makes few saints. Many of the onlookers laughed, others were indifferent, none was surprised. But presently in his mad caperings the freed man capered within reach of the waiting file, and another Burgundian promptly slipped a knife through his neck, and down he went with a death-shriek, his brilliant artery blood spurting ten feet as straight and bright as a ray of light. There was a great burst of jolly laughter all around from friend and foe alike; and thus closed one of the pleasantest incidents of my checkered military life. [WMT 18: 37]

To be sure, this vivid description of the brutalizing influence of life in the army is clearly intended as another illustration of the pernicious effect of faulty "training" upon human character. But here, apparently, there can be no real question of changing the training. In the Yankee's words, "no people in the world ever did achieve their freedom by goody-goody talk and moral suasion: it being immutable law that all revolutions that will succeed must *begin* in blood, whatever may answer afterward" (WMT 14: 171). Nor, we must suppose, can Twain's views have changed appreciably since the writing of the *Yankee*. After all, it is only on some such plea as this that he could justify Joan's having taken up arms against her fellowmen.[7]

At the heart of both books, then, lies the tragic suggestion that any active commitment to the moral experience of mankind must inevitably involve one in guilt. Of all Twain's Faustian rationalizations, this is perhaps the only one which embodies a valid ethical insight. If he had been capable of embracing it with all its implications, it might have gone far toward saving him from despair. But for those who have no faith in God, the only alternative to faith in humanity is, precisely, despair. While *Joan of Arc* is like *Faust* in dramatizing the destruction of innocence by evil, it goes far beyond the pessimism of Goethe's drama in its misanthropic suggestion that innocence has no corresponding redemptive power. Joan's martyrdom, unlike Margaret's, does not point toward any ultimate redemption. On the contrary, Twain actually discovered in it further proof that the damned human race was not worth saving.[8] When De Conte, in complaining of the failure of the French to rescue her, deplores "the littleness and meanness of our poor human race, which brags about itself so much, and thinks it is better and higher than the other animals" (WMT 18: 109), he is clearly speaking for his creator.

FIVE

JOAN AS MARTYR TO HUMAN RESPONSIBILITY

What, is great Mephistophilis so passionate
For being deprivd of the Joyes of heaven?
Learne thou of Faustus manly fortitude,
And Scorne those joyes thou never shalt possesse.
Marlowe, *The Tragicall History of Doctor Faustus*

Fürchte mich weder vor Hölle noch Teufel –
Goethe, *Faust*

In keeping with his "Gospel of Selfishness" Twain argues in "What Is Man?" that there is no such thing as "sacrifice" if that word is defined as "the doing good to another person where no shadow nor suggestion of benefit to one's self can result from it" (WIM, p. 134). Later in the same text, he applies this reasoning to "the man who stands by his duty and goes to the stake rather than be recreant to it." "It is his make and his training," he declares. "He has to content the spirit that is in him, though it cost him his life!" (WIM, p. 156).

How do these remarks apply to Joan? Did she go to the stake in order to "content her own spirit" or from some less interested motive? Judging from Twain's grandiose pronouncement that "she was perhaps the only entirely unselfish person whose name has a place in profane history" (WMT 17: xxii), one might conclude that for him her martyrdom was merely another way in which she transcended ordinary human limitations. In *Joan of Arc*, however, he did not represent that martyrdom as being wholly other-regarding. Unlike both France and Shaw, he accepted the claim made by her confessor at the trial for her rehabilitation that her immediate motive for accepting death had been to preserve her own virginity. "Did Cauchon hint to the English guards," De Conte asks after his narrative of her recantation, "that thenceforth if they chose to make their prisoner's captivity crueler and bitterer than ever, no official notice would be taken of it? Perhaps so; since the guards did begin that policy at once, and no official notice *was* taken of it. Yes, from that moment Joan's life in that dungeon was made almost unendurable. Do not ask me to enlarge upon it. I will not do it" (WMT 18: 257).

Because of Twain's long-standing obsession with sexual purity, his melodramatic insistence on this episode might easily lead the modern reader to conclude that he regarded the Maid's virginity as the only object worthy of her self-sacrifice. Yet he realized perfectly that she risked that virginity merely by adopting the career of a soldier. Thus he makes Joan predict, in the course of her interview with St. Michael in book 1, that her commitment to the cause of saving France "would give me over to insult, and rude usage, and contempt" (WMT 17: 69). Indeed her readiness to rise above the precepts of maidenly modesty actually seems to have been one of the things which he admired her for. Where Michelet, in his *Jeanne d'Arc*, claims that an English or a German girl would have been put off by the indelicacy involved in setting out across country in the company of men, Twain scoffed, "How stupid! A *Joan of Arc* would do it, no matter *what* her nationality might be. That spirit has no nationality" (p. 20, MTP).

However much Twain may have valued Joan's modesty, he must have valued something else about her more, and we can take the full measure of her heroism as he conceived it only when we have determined what it was. But we must resist the temptation to associate it with commitment to any of the political or social objectives attributed to her by his historical sources; as we have just seen, he was not sympathetic to any of those objectives. Nowhere in his writings about her does he suggest that either "the cur she had crowned" or "the nation of ingrates she had saved" was in his opinion worth dying for.[1] In a notebook entry for April 1896, he actually adduced her "treatment" as evidence bearing on the topic "Whether it were Desirable that the Human Race be Continued."[2]

For similar reasons he rejected the view of his Catholic sources that her sacrifice was motivated chiefly by religious devotion.[3] "No man that ever lived has ever done a thing to please God—primarily," he wrote in his notebook in 1899. "It was done to please himself, then God next" (MTNB, p. 365). Behind this assertion lies not only the determinist psychology he had presented in "What Is Man?" but also the whole of his long-standing Faustian quarrel with the Deity. In reaction to the claim of a Catholic priest that one benefit of Jesus' ministry had been to provide man with an object of disinterested reverence, he remarked that the very desire for such reverence argued a contemptible vanity in a God. And he added, "It was he who introduced unselfishness into the world—by offering vast rewards to people to join his following & hellfire to such as stayed out. So he introduced unselfishness by pandering to man's selfish instincts & encouraging & developing them."[4]

Thus Twain, unlike Shaw, could not wholly admire Joan either for the fervor of her religious devotion or for the soundness of her secular values. Yet he was no more inclined than Shaw to regard her death as meaningless. In a letter dated January 26, 1895, in announcing the completion of *Joan of Arc* to his friend H. H. Rogers, he remarked, "I believe I cannot let the Harpers have the Martyrdom. It is not a wig, and separable—it is the heart; it is a part of the living body, and not detachable without assassination."[5] Six years later, in a notebook sketch for an essay on the vanity of "human glory" which was to "quote the death-beds of the renowned," he wrote, "Not all sad. Washington, Franklin & others / Joan of Arc."[6]

In spite of his insistence on the pathetic aspects of Joan's martyrdom, Twain clearly perceived in it something that transcended mere pathos. If Joan had, like Goethe's Margaret, been overwhelmed by evils which she could neither resist nor comprehend, she had also confronted those evils with what struck him as extraordinary heroism. And that heroism, in his view, was no less unselfish for being, basically, neither religious nor secular but almost entirely self-regarding. Indeed, what he actually seems to have admired most in her was precisely the selflessness with which, in the interests of "contenting her own spirit," she adhered to her private ideals of conduct. While he clearly conceived of her as being too generous not to sacrifice her principles for the sake of others, yet he insisted at the same time that she was constitutionally incapable of doing so merely for her own sake. Thus, in the scene in which she repudiates her recantation, he represents her as being sustained by that same "inborn loyalty to the truth" (WMT 18: 264) which she had recently compromised on the battlefield: "She would sacrifice herself—and her *best* self; that is, her truthfulness—to save her cause; but only that; she would not buy her life at that cost. . ." (WMT 17: 118).

Twain regarded Joan's martyrdom as the "heart" of her history because he saw in it a convincing demonstration of the truth of his claim that she was an inveterately selfless, and therefore an incorruptibly virtuous, heroine. In thus idealizing her virtue, he was able to ignore both her love of God and her loyalty to France for he saw that virtue as a product of constitution rather than of commitment—of "make" rather than of "training." Indeed, it was for this reason that, in "The Turning Point of My Life," he actually described her as an unfallen figure—a still uncorrupted, and wholly unseducible Eve (WIM, p. 464). "In her," writes Roger Salomon, "his lifelong dream of Adamic innocence found a kind of religious sanction."[7] That observation enables us to place Twain's *Joan of Arc* within the context of that dialogue concerning the myth of Eve which American writers had been conducting for more than half a century.

Customarily, the technique which those writers had used in exploring that myth had been, as in the present instance, to place a morally immaculate, unfallen woman in the midst of corruption and proceed to describe the means by which she protects herself from either contamination or destruction. Customarily also, as in the case of Henry James's *The Portrait of a Lady*, they represent her as confronting the serpent directly and, through her resistance to it, developing an impressive moral maturity. But their conception of her conduct naturally varies with their conception of the role of women in the moral life. In one of the most significant versions of her career, Nathaniel Hawthorne's *The Marble Faun*, she actually retreats from the challenge of evil into moral isolation in order to remove herself from the danger of falling.

Twain in his handling of the myth was guided by the view he would soon express in "The Man That Corrupted Hadleyburg": that moral maturity depends upon the taking of ethical risks. And the fact that, in taking such risks, Joan was led to compromise her principles, merely provided him with another demonstration of her unfaltering moral heroism. His attitude toward her commitment was conditioned throughout by the Goethean view that it is through action in the world alone—however grave may be the spiritual perils to which it exposes one—that man can work out his redemption. "There are several good protections against temptation," he wrote in his notebook in 1895, "but the surest is cowardice."[8] In the short story "Was It Heaven? Or Hell?", in rebuking two conventionally virtuous old ladies who refuse to tell benevolent lies lest they be damned for it, Twain's protagonist fumes, "Reform! Drop this mean and sordid and selfish devotion to the saving of your shabby little souls, and hunt up something to do that's got some dignity to it! *Risk* your souls! risk them in good causes; then if you lose them, why should you care? Reform!"[9]

Thus the same sort of moral courage which had enabled Joan to deceive the Burgundian captain accounted for another quality in her which Twain admired: her Faustian superiority to the fear of hell. Without this quality, he apparently believed, she could not have conducted herself effectively at her trial, because the fear of excommunication would have caused her to recant. "I could see the red waves tossing in that shoreless lake of fire," he makes De Conte remark, "I could see the black myriads of the damned rise out of them and struggle and sink and rise again; and I knew that Joan was seeing what I saw. . . ." But in spite of her horror at the prospect, the page goes on, Joan stood her ground, for "Joan of Arc was not made as others are made. Fidelity to principle, fidelity to truth, fidelity to her word, all these were in her bone and in her flesh—they were parts of her. She could not change, she could not cast them out. . . . Where she had taken her stand and planted her foot, there she would abide; hell itself could not move her from that place" (WMT 18: 214-15).

This is a remarkably heroic passage, especially coming from one who in part believed that he himself was going to hell. [10] Indeed, in Twain's eyes this willingness to risk damnation for a generous purpose raised Joan even above Jesus, in whose failure to do so he discoverd an abject inability to rise above mere self-seeking. But he did not believe that the willingness to take such a risk was proof of a transcendent selflessness. In a notebook entry dated March 30, 1896, he attacked the argument that Jesus' charity in dying for man's sins was a convincing proof of his divinity. "Millions of men and millions of women have done more," he declared; "they have freely given their lives to save even individuals who were in danger—and risked eternal damnation when they did it; for they rushed to the rescue without first squaring up their sin-account with God. Every volunteer in the army offers his life to save his country or his country's honor, and does it on the chance that his death may land him in hell, not on the Great White Throne, which was Christ's sure destination" (MTNB, pp. 289-90).

Twain frequently went farther than this, pointing out that moral rebels have sometimes been willing to defy damnation even when they firmly believed that their conduct was actually making it inevitable. Indeed, that observation lies at the heart of one of the most impressive episodes in his fiction: the scene in which Huckleberry Finn makes up his mind to go to hell rather than turn Jim over to Mrs. Watson. In the same year in which he finished *Joan of Arc,* he commented at length on that episode in another notebook entry which throws a good deal of light on his attitude toward the Maid's commitment.

Twain explains that as part of "an elaborate & formidable lay sermon on morals & the conduct of life & things of that stately sort," he intends to make use of Huck's private rebellion against the slave-holding ethic of his time to "exploit the proposition that in a crucial moral emergency a sound heart is a safer guide than in ill-trained conscience. I sh'd support this doctrine," he continues, "with a chapter from a book of mine where a sound heart & a deformed conscience come into collision & conscience suffers defeat." After describing the chapter in some detail, he adds that the very existence of a belief in "the awful sacredness of slave property" among the down-trodden of the community "shows that that strange thing, the conscience—that unerring monitor—can be trained to approve any wild thing you *want* it to approve if you begin its education early & stick to it."[11]

Clearly, then, the Faustian conviction that the idea of hell encourages moral cowardice and moral conservatism was reinforced in Twain's case by the Romantic-radical view that, since men are corrupted by their training, their only hope of redemption lies in their temperament. Hence it is not surprising that he should have reserved his deepest admiration for those who by "a law of their make" are too generous to regard the fear of the Lord as the beginning of wisdom. If the damned human race can be saved by anyone, he implies, it can only be by one who, unlike Jesus, is willing to risk being damned himself.

SIX

THE GREAT DARK

> *When he asked what Doctor Faustus desired of him,*
> *Faustus asked whether it could not be arranged for a spirit*
> *to conduct him into Hell and out again, so that he might*
> *see and mark the nature, fundament, quality and sub-*
> *stance of hell.*
>
> *The History of Doctor Johann Faustus* (anon.)

Although *Joan of Arc* is the longest and most ambitious of Twain's attempts to deal with the subject of religious heroism, it is by no means either the most effective or the most Faustian. Both of those distinctions belong without doubt to an unfinished novel called *The Great Dark*, the idea for which seems, characteristically, to have come to him in a dream. In a notebook entry for August 10, 1898, he wrote, "Last night dreamed of a whaling cruise in a drop of water. Not by microscope, but actually. This would mean a reduction of the participants to a minuteness which would make them nearly invisible to God, and He wouldn't be interested in them any longer" (MTNB, p. 365).

The narrative begins with a curious variant of the bargain with the devil. The protagonist, Henry Edwards, has been so impressed by the teeming life which appears in a waterdrop viewed through his children's toy microscope that he conceives the wild idea of becoming the Columbus of this as yet unnavigated waterway. "An ocean in a drop of water—" he muses, "and unknown, uncharted, unexplored by man! By man, who gives all his time to the Africas and the poles, with this unsearched marvelous world right at his elbow" (WWD, p. 104). At this moment, with suspiciously perfect timing, the Superintendent of Dreams appears.

Just how Edwards happened to involve himself with this oddly sinister, supernatural figure is not clear from Twain's narrative as it stands. Their acquaintance seems, in any case, to have been of some continuance; for when the Superintendent warns Edwards that the adventure he is contemplating will be perilous, the latter's vainglorious response is, "It is no matter; you have seen me face dangers before—" (WWD, p. 105). And we may also presume that in offering to provide Edwards with a ship and crew suitable for his purposes, the Superintendent of Dreams is impelled by no generous motive. For in the world of the water drop he actually appears as the Superintendent of Realities—a description which, together with his Mephistophelian love of practical jokes, and his faculty for diabolical laughter, subtly betrays his essentially satanic character.[1]

The immediate effect upon Edwards of this highly questionable arrangement proves to be deeply unsettling. He suddenly finds himself with his wife and two children in the midst of a vast and turbulent ocean—an ocean infested by strange and frightening monsters and brooded over by a perpetual starless night. He has not been at sea for more than a few hours before he learns that both captain and crew are unnerved because the ship seems to be hopelessly lost. There are no heavenly bodies visible by which to fix its position, and the landmarks whose presence is demanded by the ships reckoning have apparently disappeared. Moreover, in spite of his privileged knowledge of their situation, Edwards's own sense of disorientation and bewilderment is by no means inferior to that of the crew. Memories of his former life "at sea" recur to him as the voyage progresses, but no one can give him any idea where the ship has sailed from, and, as he alone knows, the Antarctic toward which it is supposedly voyaging simply does not exist.

In short, Edwards's "dream" turns almost immediately into a frightening nightmare. And as Twain further developed it in his notes, it became more nightmarish still. The crew were to speak another ship at sea, to learn that it was filled with treasure, and to pursue it into a deadly region known as the "The Great White Glare"—a region of perpetual burning heat created by the light from the microscope's reflector. At that point virtually everyone on board, including Edwards's own wife and children (who were clearly modeled on Livy, Susy, and Jean Clemens), would perish in a series of cataclysmic disasters reminiscent of the horrors of the Wrath to Come.[2]

Doubtless Twain's handling of these disasters would have been quite revealing; yet even without them the significance of the work emerges with startling clarity. It is a vision of life as a voyage in "the Great Dark"—a voyage without either destination or port of origin, pursued in a ship which drifts aimlessly from point to meaningless point through a darkness lit only by the promise of impending disaster. In the world of such a ship, Twain seems to be saying, aspiration is a mockery, heroism a form of futility, and love merely a trap set by a mindlessly cruel destiny for the torture and enthrallment of the unwary. For the ship is a "derelict": it has been abandoned by God, Twain's Mephistopheles, like Faust's, having led him on a journey through hell.

This surely is one of Twain's most compelling and powerful metaphors. Yet, oddly enough, he seems to have been unwilling to accept its implications. The work in its unfinished form concludes with an act of religious heroism whose absurdity somehow renders it only the more impressive. At one point in the narrative the crew, having been thrown into a panic by the uncanny character of the voyage, is persuaded by an unscrupulous ship's carpenter to rebel against the officers. The situation is saved through the courage and resourcefulness of the captain—a man who is described as being "remarkably and sincerely and persistently pious" (WWD, p. 147), and who, after restoring order, proceeds to encourage his men with the following spirited harangue:

> Are we men—grown men. . .men made in the image of God and ready to do when He commands and die when He calls—or are we just sneaks and curs and carpenters!". . .*I* don't know where this ship is, but she's in the hands of God, and that's enough for me, it's enough for you, and it's enough for anybody but a carpenter. If it is God's will that we pull through, we pull through—otherwise not. We haven't had an observation for four months, but we are going ahead, and do our best to fetch up somewhere. [WWD, p. 150]

Here the manuscript breaks off. I would like to believe that Twain's failure to continue resulted from his inability to answer the questions which he raised in this passage. To what extent, for instance, should we allow our admiration for Captain Davis's heroic resolve to be qualified by our awareness of its futility? Knowing as he could not that there was simply no place to "fetch up" at, would we behave as he did? Or would we allow the mutinous carpenter to take over the ship?

At any rate, Twain could not have concluded his book at a more impressive moment. Not only is Captain Davis one of the most compelling symbolic figures in his fiction but he is also one of the most universal. For his case, after all, is exactly ours. His ignorance is our ignorance, his confusion our confusion, and the Great Dark into which he makes his heroic leap of faith persists as a troubling challenge to our own baffled souls.

PART II

ANATOLE FRANCE & THE MAID

A Naturalist View

But the time will come when you yourself, overcome by the priests' terrifying words, will seek to free yourself from us; and naturally, for how many empty tales can they fashion for you, able to overthrow your reasoned plans for life and to confuse in fear all your fortunes! They act with reason, for if men were to see that there is a fixed end to their troubles, they would be able to find some way of resisting the threats that the priests base upon man's religious scruples. . . .

This terror, this darkness of the soul, must be dispelled neither by the rays of the sun, nor by the bright weapons of the day, but by an understanding of nature's outer form and inner laws.

Lucretius, *De Rerum Natura, bk. 1*

ONE

FRANCE AND NATURALISM

> *Incredulity– let us remember it–is the foundation of all wisdom according to Aristotle. This maxim is a very good one for anyone who reads history, and especially the history of ages past.*
> Voltaire, *History of Charles XII,* 1748 preface.

Anatole France's life of the Maid, *Vie de Jeanne d'Arc*, was first published, after twenty-five years of research, in 1908.[1] In many ways it was a surprising book for the aging Frenchman to write. Apart from critical monographs, it represents his only ambitious attempt at historical biography, and, being well over twice as long as anything else in his canon, it sins notably against that conciseness which he elsewhere describes as the mark of the true French genius.[2] But what at first sight appears most surprising in *Vie de Jeanne d'Arc* is its air of objectivity. Abandoning for the most part that philosophical subjectivism which was characteristic of him, France here assumes the detachment appropriate to the natural scientist. In fact, the perspective adopted throughout is that of philosophical Naturalism.

According to the conception of such Naturalism that was current in France's lifetime, all Naturalists believe in the autonomy of natural processes, but they differ in their reactions to the problem of creation and to the "argument from design" for the existence of God. An article in the *Grand Dictionnaire Universel*, published by Larousse in the last half of the nineteenth century, distinguishes two types of Naturalism. Considered from the point of view of creation theory, it asserts, Naturalism is the doctrine that nature is a self-regulating system owing neither its origin nor its continuation in being to any non-natural source. By this definition, it is fully consistent with virtually all forms of materialistic monism, including Pantheism. The second definition, however, confines Naturalism to the doctrine that all natural processes proceed from physical laws and are thus completely independent of non-natural forces. So conceived, Naturalism need not deny the existence of God, though it does deny that He interferes in the order of His creation, either by performing miracles or by extending grace to favored individuals.[3] By the first of these definitions, Naturalism would include materialists and monists of such widely differing persuasions as Diderot and Renan; by the second, it would include deists like Voltaire.

France admired all three of these thinkers and, in fact, had no quarrel with Naturalist cosmology. But he was unable to accept the epistemology which has been derived from it. Since the Enlightenment virtually all Naturalists have held that the sole viable means of enquiry into the nature of reality is the so-called scientific method;[4] France, following the ancient philosopher Pyrrho, rejected scientific rationalism on the skeptical grounds that reality is absolutely unknowable.

Naturalism developed in France as a reaction not only against Catholicism but also against the Pyrrhonist Skepticism of Michel de Montaigne. In his *Apology for Raymond Sebond,* Montaigne pointed to the failure of science to account for the motions of the heavenly bodies, and complained that scientists' confusion about the macrocosm was mirrored in their descriptions of the microcosm: "There is no more retrogradation, trepidation, accession, recession, reversal, in the stars and heavenly bodies, than they have fabricated in this poor little human body. . . . To accommodate the impulses they see in man. . .into how many parts have they divided our soul?"[5] Well before Montaigne wrote this, however, these problems of celestial mechanics had been substantially solved by the heliocentric theory of Copernicus, and the greatest of French Naturalists, Voltaire, in his *Traité de métaphysique,* took advantage of that fact to invert Montaigne's argument. The problems of astronomy can be dealt with, he observed, by imagining oneself in the sphere of the sun, and thus "away from the globe of the earth, from the surface of which the celestial motions appear irregular and confused." Similarly, the scientific student of man must place himself "hors de sa sphere," thereby stripping himself of all the prejudices which may result from personal, national, or sectarian self-interest.[6] By applying scientific detachment to the humanities, Voltaire implied, the savant might hope to achieve in them a revolution comparable to that which Copernicus had accomplished in astronomy.

France disagreed. He believed, like Montaigne, that the subjective character of perception makes it impossible for the scientist to learn anything about objective reality. Hence, he argued, the substitution of the Copernican theory for the Ptolemaic is merely the substitution of one illusion for another.[7] And the historian is even worse off than the scientist, for whatever he may propose, he cannot hope to strip himself of all his prejudices. He must concern himself with notable facts, and must decide what is notable "arbitrarily, according to his own taste and character, after his own fancy—in short, as an artist."[8]

Nevertheless, in the preface to *Vie de Jeanne d'Arc* France denies that he personally has been guilty of any such subjectivism. After asserting that "a terrible temptation for the historian of such a history is to throw himself into the battle," he then boasts of his firmness in resisting that temptation: "I have composed this history with an ardent and tranquil zeal. I have sought the truth without self-interest, I have encountered it without fear." (15:67-68).

Such zeal on behalf of historical truth appears surprising in one who held, with his own Jérôme Coignard, that "history is condemned by a natural defect to the indeterminacy of falsehood."[9] But classical Skepticism is scarcely consistent with philosophical rigor, and, like most Pyrrhonists, France was prevented both by irrationalism and by a temperamental abhorrence of dogma from any attempt to subject his ideas to a rational discipline. "Just as a great country possesses the most diverse climates," he once wrote, "so there is scarcely any expansive soul which does not embrace numerous contradictions. In truth, souls exempt from all illogicality frighten me. Being unable to imagine that they are never deceived, I fear that they may always be; whereas a mind which does not pique itself on its logic can always find the truth again after having lost it."[10]

But the ambiguities implicit in France's views about historiography are not entirely owing to this Pyrrhonist irrationalism. The critic of his work can discover in nearly all of it a tendency, rooted deeply in the nature of the man, to vacillate between an intense temperamental love of illusion and an equally intense temperamental need for reality. In a passage in *Les Opinions de M. Jérôme Coignard*, France indicates that he was aware of this tendency, and that he cultivated it for its own aesthetic interest.

This passage is an ironic eulogy of the title character, an eighteenth-century abbé whose ideas on most subjects bear a striking resemblance to those of his creator. It begins by observing of him that "in order to astonish and enrapture mankind by a vast and beautiful intellectual edifice, he only wanted the facility, or the desire, to stuff a profusion of sophisms, like cement, into the interstices between truths." Yet because of this failure in "l'esprit de système," it continues, he was bound to appear as "a sort of marvelous amalgam of Epicurus and St. Francis of Assisi":

> Epicurus freed souls from empty fears and instructed them to proportion their ideas of happiness to their wretched nature and feeble powers. Good St. Francis, tenderer and more sensual, conducted them to bliss through interior revery, and strove that, by his example, souls might expand in delight in the depths of an enchanted solitude. Both of them were benevolent: the one for destroying illusions which deceive, the other for creating illusions from which one does not awaken. [8:314-15]

This satiric self-portrait is clearly intended as a caricature. But the ambivalence toward illusion it expresses is characteristic of France, and, in keeping with his claim that history must reflect the historian's "own taste and character," it profoundly influenced his *Vie de Jeanne d'Arc*.

Indeed, the work seems originally to have been conceived as a means of uniting the appeal of illusion to that of reality. In an early essay on the Maid, "Sur Jeanne d'Arc," France argued that her triumph had resulted from the religious reverence in which she was held by her followers, and was thus quite literally a triumph of faith. Hence the historian who would treat her career naturalistically must "examine by what slow and deep travail the Christian spirit formed the idea of the power of virginity, and how the cult of Mary and the legends of the saints prepared minds for the advent of a Catherine of Sienna and of a Joan of Arc."[11] The biographer of the Maid, he implied, can achieve realism only by immersing himself in romance.

In this conviction France was evidently emulating his friend and mentor, Ernest Renan. In 1890, in an article in praise of Renan's *History of the Origins of Christianity,* he observed, "The subject demanded the rarest qualities of intelligence, and even the most contradictory. It required a critical sense always on the alert, a scientific skepticism capable of setting at naught all the guile of the faithful, and their ingenuousness, more potent than their guile. It required at the same time a lively affection for the divine, a secret instinct for the needs of the human soul, and what might be called an objective piety."[12] In short, Renan had to be "a sort of marvelous amalgam of Epicurus and St. Francis of Assisi."

France concluded this essay by congratulating himself for living at a time "when science and poetry each finds its account, since an enlightened criticism displays together, in marvelous fashion, both the sap-filled stem of reality and the full-blown flower of legend." In another early essay on the Maid, "Jeanne d'Arc et la poésie," he suggests that he intended his biography of her to be a celebration of the creative power of myth. "Joan is made entirely of poetry," he wrote. She sprang from poetry, popular and Christian, from the litanies of the virgin and the Golden Legend, from the marvelous stories of those brides of Jesus Christ who drew, over the white robe of virginity, the red robe of martyrdom. . . . She sprang from the great thought which made a rose of fire bloom above the portals of our churches; she sprang from the prophecies through which the poor folk of the kingdom of France foretold a better future; she sprang from the ecstacy and tears of an entire people who, in a time of wretchedness, like Mary of Avignon, beheld arms in the sky and trusted thereafter only in her weakness."[13]

One consequence of this approach is that France's book is filled with antiquarian lore, including saints' lives, popular legends, and apocryphal historical narratives in order to provide the reader with a sense of that medieval world view which had made Joan's emergence possible. "The first task of the historian," Renan writes, "is to sketch carefully the milieu in which the event he relates occurred."[14] But France, unlike Renan, was unable to sustain that "lively instinct for the divine" which had originally attracted him to his subject. By the turn of the century he had become deeply contemptuous of the faith of St. Francis, and that ultimately led him to adopt a condescending attitude toward the Middle Ages. "If we truly want to live in the fifteenth century," he explains in his preface to *Vie de Jeanne d'Arc*, "how many things we must forget: sciences, manners, all the acquisitions which make us moderns. We must forget that the earth is round and that the stars are suns, and not lamps suspended from a crystal vault, forget the cosmology of Laplace in order to believe only in the science of St. Thomas, of Dante, and of those cosmographers of the Middle Ages who teach us the creation in seven days. . . ." The biographer of the maid still requires double vision. Now, however, France characterizes what he needs to understand her point of view not as "objective piety," but as "ignorance" (15:63).

The principal cause of this change of heart was the Dreyfus affair, which produced an international scandal in 1897. "L'Affaire," as it is still called in France, involved a conspiracy on the part of the French military establishment to protect one of its members by blaming his crime on a young Jewish officer. The role played by the anti-Jewish French church in enflaming popular sentiment against Dreyfus made

France painfully aware of the potentially destructive character of "illusions which deceive."[15] Since both the clergy and the army had been supporters of the Maid in her lifetime, France's book about her had begun to take on the character of an anti-establishment crusade even before she was beatified in 1905. "Aren't they talking about canonizing the holy girl?" he asked his secretary, Jean-Jacques Brousson. "We're in a steeplechase. We must finish our liberal and republican monument before the priests perch her on their altars. There's no time to lose."[16]

Thus *Vie de Jeanne d'Arc* became imbued with an anti-religious bias which had formed no part of its original conception, and which tended to confirm France's view that history cannot be otherwise than subjective. "One feels antipathies at work in his book," Shaw remarked in the preface to *Saint Joan*. "He is not anti-Joan; but he is anti-clerical, anti-mystic, and fundamentally unable to believe that there ever was any such person as the real Joan."

No Naturalist would accept Shaw's implication that an anti-mystical approach to history is necessarily a biased one. But, biased or not, even France's Naturalism betrays the influence of "his own taste and character." His handling of the Maid's claim to divine inspiration, for instance, reveals no trace of that "objective piety" which he had once praised in Renan. "There is nothing more inconstant nor more contradictory," he asserts in *Vie de Jeanne d'Arc*, "than the inspirations of these visionaries, the playthings of their dreams" (16:73).

Moreover, France's Pyrrhonism carried him much further than his mentor in repudiating the supernatural. As hostile to the dogmatism of science as to that of religion, he vigorously rejected Renan's claim that miracles would be acceptable in history if they could be scientifically verified. To suppose that such verification is even conceivable is to attribute to the scientist "a complete and absolute knowledge of the facts of nature, such as he does not have and never will, and such as no one on earth ever has had."[17] Following Montaigne, he argued that the only way science can avoid mistaking for impossible what is really only unusual is to abandon all preconceptions on that subject. "It is possible that there are phenomena which are peculiar, uncommon, subtle, and of indeterminate production. Formal science must run the risk of ignoring them altogether if it waits for them to turn up in its retorts."[18]

Consequently, France's handling of allegedly miraculous episodes is very different from Renan's. Where Renan would denounce such episodes as either fabrications or frauds, France records nearly all the miracles attributed to the Maid with an air of studied detachment. At the same time, however, he makes skilled use of his antiquarian researches to define the context of superstition within which those miracles occurred, and by this means he encourages his readers to attribute them to a natural origin.

One such episode concerns a still-born child which the Maid claimed to have restored to life at the village of Lagny. France describes the ideas of the medieval church on the fate of unbaptized infants, arguing from the evidence of contemporary chronicles that resurrections of such infants occurred frequently at this time. Joan must have been familiar with "this sort of miracle," he reasons, since there was, within forty miles of Domremy, a church dedicated to "Our Lady of the Aviots," who was celebrated for bringing unbaptized infants back to life. "If we are to believe the tales that were circulated about this episode," France concludes, "the child had not given any sign of life for three days after its birth, but the gossips of Lagny had doubtless exaggerated the number of hours during which it had remained inert, like those good dames who, from an egg laid by the husband of one of their number, had fabricated a hundred before the end of the day" (16:45-49).

The passage evidently implies that the child was comatose, and that the failure of the Maid and her companions to perceive that fact should be regarded as an effect of superstition acting upon a deeply religious mind.[19] With the first proposition, Renan would probably have agreed. "In our time," he declares, "have we not seen nearly all the fashionable people taken in by clumsy enchantments and puerile illusions? Marvelous exploits which have been vouched for by entire villages have proven, thanks to a more rigorous enquiry, worthy of condemnation" (HOC 1: xcvi). But unlike France, Renan does not regard his hero as the credulous victim of his own legend: he represents the raising of Lazarus as a calculated act of deceit on Jesus' part, and in the preface to the thirteenth edition of *Vie de Jésus* he gives Joan credit for a similar astuteness: "Did not Joan of Arc more than once make her voices speak according to the need of the moment? If the story of the secret revelation that she made to King Charles VII has any reality, which would be difficult to deny, that innocent girl must have presented as the effect of a super-natural intuition what she had learned in confidence" (HOC 1: xxiv-xxv).[20]

Moreover, although superficially more intolerant, the master's Naturalism is actually less inflexible than that of his disciple. True,

France's carefully chosen word *inert* (the authorized English translation has *comatose*) leaves open the possibility that the Maid may really
have performed such a "marvel." But even if she had, France would
still refuse to describe the feat as a miracle. "Though we were to see a
dead man restored to life," he declares in "Sur le Miracle," "the
miracle would not be proven unless we knew the true nature of life
and of death, and that we never will know" (9:489)[21]

In adopting this position, France made himself vulnerable to the
usual anti-Naturalist objection: there can be no proof that miracles
never occur; hence, by ruling them out dogmatically, Naturalists are
being false to their own skeptical creed.[22] Within a year of the publication of *Vie de Jeanne d'Arc* the Scottish historian Andrew Lang used
this argument to attack the book for its thesis that the Maid had been
misled by superstition. In the preface to his rival biography, also
published in 1908, Lang complained that in casting doubt on the
Maid's credibility France was, in effect, treating his sources "arbitrarily, according to his own taste and character, after his own fancy." "To
reject abundance of sworn evidence," Lang protested, "because it
conflicts with a critic's personal idea of what is probable or possible is
not the method of History, and will not be adopted in this book. Much
less will I reject, for instance, the evidence of Jeanne herself on any
point, and give a fanciful theory of my own as to what really occurred." Moreover, Lang contended, by rejecting testimony for phenomena which were "peculiar, uncommon, subtle, and of indeterminate production," France had implicitly attributed to science "a complete and absolute knowledge of the facts of nature." "If there are
incidents in her career," he went on, "which science, so far, cannot
explain, I shall not therefore regard them as false. Science may be able
to explain them on some future day; at present she is not
omniscient."[23]

It may be doubted, however, whether an uncritical acceptance of
"sworn evidence" is in fact the method of history. It is one thing to
claim that since science is not omniscient it cannot verify a miracle; it
is another to argue on that basis that it is illegitimate to criticize
historical sources in the light of available data. "Man must not be
deterred," Voltaire asserts, "from searching for what is useful to him
by any consideration that he cannot know everything." [24] In this
matter France's Naturalism is fully consistent with his Pyrrhonism,
for a skeptical refusal to reject the marvelous does not entail a credulous acceptance of it. "It seems to me," writes Montaigne, "that we
may be pardoned for disbelieving a marvel, at least as long as we can

turn aside and avoid the supernatural explanation by nonmarvelous means."[25]

France revealed his views a year after the publication of *Vie de Jeanne d'Arc* in the preface to a burlesque saint's life, *The Miracle of Saint Nicholas the Great*. In a long passage probably intended as an attack on the critics of his biography of the Maid, he demonstrates how effectively he could exploit the mask of faith to expound the doctrine of skepticism. According to the text of a celebrated ballad, he relates, a wicked innkeeper once cut three little children to pieces and pickled them in a salting tub, leaving them to soak for seven years. Ordinarily, he observes, this last detail would puzzle the judicious historian: the usual practice is to remove the pieces of pickled meat from the tub at the end of about six weeks. In this case, however, the text is explicit: it was seven years before the good saint, entering the inn late at night, drove the wicked innkeeper out into the darkness. Only then, by laying his hands on the tub, did he bring the three children back to life.

"Such, in substance," France concludes, "is the narrative of this forgotten chronicler. Skepticism must surely appear ill-advised when it strikes at the most vital traditions of popular sensibility."[26]

TWO

JOAN AS VICTIM OF NERVOUS DISORDER

The great subverter of Pyrrhonism *or the excessive principles of scepticism is action, and employment, and the occupations of common life. These principles may flourish and triumph in the schools; where it is, indeed, difficult, if not impossible, to refute them. But as soon as they leave the shade, and by the presence of the real objects, which actuate our passions and sentiments, are put in opposition to the more powerful principles of our nature, they vanish like smoke, and leave the most determined sceptic in the same condition as other mortals.*
Hume, *An Enquiry Concerning Human Understanding*

He reasoned like a madman, and behaved like everybody else.

Diderot, *Encyclopedia,* s.v. "Pyrrhonienne"

Whatever skeptical misgivings France may have had about dogmatically rejecting Joan's "miracles," he abandoned them in dealing with her voices; his antiquarian researches had convinced him that Sts. Catherine and Margaret were wholly imaginary beings. "There is an absurd impiety," remarks the Abbé Jerôme Coignard in *At the Sign of the Queen Pedauque,* "in the pretention that God granted an appearance to this Joan Dulys of saints who have never existed."[1] Although the problem of determining the nature of Joan's saints was thus solved for France at the outset, he confesses that he personally was not able to provide a natural explanation for them. For that reason he applied for a professional opinion to his friend Dr. Georges Dumas, a neuropathologist at the Sorbonne (15: 30).

Dumas's reply, which France prints in an appendix, suggests that there were serious limitations in the kind of psychological knowledge that was readily available to Naturalist historians shortly after the turn of the century. Nowhere does Dumas indicate any awareness that hallucinations may be purely psychogenic. Rather, he apparently takes it for granted that Sts. Catherine and Margaret were produced through the action on Joan's nervous system of some form of organic pathology. In one passage he speculates that she may have induced them by fasting, and elsewhere he attempts to relate them to the claim made by her squire, Jean d'Aulon, that she never menstruated. (16: 443-44). But the hypothesis that he apparently finds most attractive is that she was suffering from hysteria related to a hemi-anaesthesia of the right side—a conjecture which he bases in part on the observation of the great French neuropathologist Charcot that "unilateral halluci-nations of the sight are common in cases of hysteria" (16: 444). Actu-ally, sixteen years earlier Sigmund Freud had argued that hysterical symptoms are produced not by nervous disorder but autosuggestively as an effect of subconscious repression.[2] In spite of Freud's findings, however, very few specialists in 1908 were inclined to recognize any direct relation between hysterical hallucination and psychic disturbance.[3] Dumas himself explicitly denied that any such relation obtained in the case of the Maid. "If hysteria did affect her," he declares at one point, "it was only to permit the most secret emotions of her heart to objectify themselves in the form of visions and celestial voices. . . . It fortified her faith, consecrated her mission, but, in her intelligence, in her will, she remained healthy and upright. . ." (16: 447).

Long before France wrote his *Vie de Jeanne d'Arc*, he betrayed his ignorance of the psychic origin of hallucinations in an article called "Madmen in Literature." There, after observing that "madness, when it is not characterized by any anatomical lesion, remains indefinable," he declares, "We say that a man is mad when he does not think as we do. That is all." In support of that view, he cited Joan of Arc as one who, like Socrates, had combined greatness of mind with a tendency to hallucinate.[4]

But France did not confine his argument to the misconception that hallucinations result merely from an abnormality in nervous organi-zation and may therefore appear without detriment to either the will or the intellect. In the same essay he advanced the Pyrrhonist view that since all our perceptions are necessarily subjective, they cannot give us any information about objective reality and, therefore, the distinction between hallucination and objective perception has no basis in fact: "And anyway, are we not all visionaries and *hallucinés?* Do we know anything whatever about the external world? Do we perceive anything in our entire lives but the luminous or sonorous vibrations of our sensory nerves?" (6: 171).

In that seedbed of Enlightenment Skepticism, Pierre Bayle's *Historical and Critical Dictionary*, Bayle identifies as "Pyrrhonian" the principle "that the absolute and internal nature of objects is hidden from us and that we can only be sure of how they appear to us in various respects." Bayle attributes this last idea to a philosophical abbé, who explains that none of the properties of bodies can be proven to exist anywhere but in the mind which perceives them. "I could therefore," he concludes, "feel heat and cold, see colors and shapes, extension and motion, even though there were no bodies in the universe. I have therefore no good proof of the existence of bodies."[5]

This paradox, as presented by Bayle, is intended to demonstrate the folly of relying for guidance on our feeble human reason rather than on Christian faith.[6] In response, modern Naturalists have tended to argue that normal perception differs from hallucination in ways which can best be explained by premising that it refers to an external reality. The rationalist thinkers of the Enlightenment, anticipating this view, insisted on the absurdity of behaving as if all phenomena were hallucinatory. This is the position of the article "Pyrrhonienne" in Diderot's *Encyclopedia*. "They say that [Pyrrho's]conduct was in keeping with his philosophy; that he took no precautions whatever; that he walked straight toward a chariot, toward a precipice, toward a stake, toward a ferocious beast; that he defied on the most perilous occasions the manifest testimony of his senses. . . ." If this were so, the article concludes, we would be compelled to regard Pyrrho as a madman. "But it is not so at all: he reasoned like a madman, and behaved like everybody else."[7]

In answer to such objections, the Pyrrhonists claimed that to treat phenomena as if they were real does not logically entail a belief in their reality. "In fact," France declares, "reality or appearance, it is all one. To love or to suffer in this world images suffice. It is not necessary that their objectivity be demonstrated."[8] But Enlightenment Naturalists were not impressed by this piece of casuistry. "We will only have to change a single word in our discourses," writes Voltaire in his *Traité de métaphysique*. "When, for example, some battles have been given, we will have to say that ten thousand men appear to have been killed, that such-and-such an officer seems to have had his leg broken, and that a surgeon appears to have cut it off. Similarly, when we are hungry we will ask for the appearance of a piece of bread in order to make a show of digesting it."[9]

In spite of such criticism, skeptical subjectivism exerted a profound influence on European cultural history throughout the eighteenth and nineteenth centuries. Popularized by Berkeley and Hume in England,

and by Montaigne and Descartes in France, it became so widespread that there is really no need to ask where France came by it: it was in the air. Thus in various articles in *La Vie littéraire* he attributes it to a number of distinguished contemporaries, including Jules Lemaître, Leconte de Lisle, Maurice Barrès, Prosper Merimée. Many of those who did not embrace the doctrine directly were affected by it through its influence on the Romantic movement; for by undermining the classical distinction between appearance and reality, it fostered Romantic subjectivism, and encouraged the notion that the imagination rather than the reason is the best interpreter of experience.[10]

Accordingly, Romantic writers in general tended to be tolerant of hallucination, even regarding it as a possible source of supramundane enlightenment. The French historian Michelet, after asserting that Joan's voices resulted because she was incompletely developed sexually, characterized them as the productions of a kind of creative genius comparable to that of the great poets:

> She was a living legend. . . . But the vital force in her, exalted and concentrated, became all the more creative. Unawares, the young girl *created*, so to speak, her own ideas, turned them into realities, made them entities, powers, imparted to them, from the treasure of her virginal life, an existence so splendid, so compelling that the paltry realities of this world grew faint in comparison.
> If *poetry* means *creation*, this no doubt is supreme poetry.[11]

In *The Apostles*, Renan carried a comparable attitude toward hallucination to a similarly escapist conclusion. Asserting that the doctrine of the resurrection had its source in the imagination of St. Mary Magdalene, he denounced that "impotent reason" which would venture "to apply a cold analysis to this masterpiece of idealism and of love." "If wisdom," he declared, "declines to console this poor human race, betrayed by destiny, then let madness try its luck."[12]

Neither Michelet nor Renan, however, valued hallucinations merely as such. A corollary to their Romantic approach is that the value of a given hallucination will depend upon the nature of the imagination which produces it. In a conversation with his friend Loyson which took place shortly before the publication of *Vie de Jeanne d'Arc*, France made this point in defense of his claim that the Maid's voices were not evidence of madness: "In the fifteenth century the minds of all were haunted by chimeras. If Joanie *saw her voices*, as she naively remarked, her judges, who wanted to convict her of witchcraft, had an inflexible faith in demons. But whereas Joan's dreams were radiant and incited her to the noblest enterprises, those of her torturers were disgusting, infamous, and monstrous."[13]

In short, France came ultimately to adopt the view that whether or not hallucinations should be taken as evidence of mental derangement must depend on their character and behavior. This was precisely the position adopted by Shaw in the preface to *Saint Joan*. But Shaw bases his admiration for Joan's voices on the realist argument that they gave her accurate and useful information. France, by contrast, declared, "Her perpetual hallucinations made her more often than not incapable of distinguishing truth from falsehood" (15: 5). His motive for admiring Joan's saints, unlike Shaw's, was almost wholly escapist and hence his description of them as "radiant."[14] And the relation that his taste for such radiance bears to his philosophical subjectivism is revealed by his attack on Zola in "George Sand and Idealism in Art": "Well, then, since each of the evidences that we receive from nature possesses just as little objective reality as the others, since all of the images that we fashion of things correspond, not to the things themselves, but entirely to the states of our souls, why should we not by preference seek out and enjoy the images of grace, of beauty, and of love?" (6: 304).

Thus the same Pyrrhonist argument that Bayle had used to discredit reason in the interest of faith was pressed by France into the service of a decadent Aestheticism. Although France, like many of his contemporaries, longed for hallucinations as a means of escape from the monotony of the quotidian, he was temperamentally too much of a rationalist not to regard them with suspicion. He had once criticized an orthodox biography of Jesus by remarking that one cannot write history and accept the supernatural, since "history consists entirely in the effort to discover the natural sequence of events."[15] In fact his biography of the Maid cannot be said to bear out the anti-Naturalist stance which he assumes in the essay on George Sand.

Because France did not share Shaw's belief in inspiration, he denied emphatically that Joan's voices could have offered her any constructive advice. Indeed, he seems to have reasoned that, inasmuch as they necessarily shared her ignorance and inexperience, they were bound to let her down just when she stood most in need of reliable counsel. He claims that when she was at Orleans she had a dream in which her voices ordered her to attack the English but neglected to inform her where they were. "What had occurred on this occasion," he observes, "is what always did occur. The saints had told her only what she herself knew; they had not revealed a thing to her about what she needed to learn; they had not informed her that at that very moment the French were attacking the Bastille Saint Loup and were suffering great hurt. And they went away, the blessed ones, leaving her in error and ignorance about what was happening, and in uncertainty about what she had to do" (15: 391-92). [16]

Nor was the misconduct of the saints limited to such minor truancies. More damaging still to the Maid was the conviction they fostered in her that she had the backing of God, because it made her at once dangerously unrealistic and fatuously overconfident. "Being a prophetess," France declares, "she was like every prophetess in this: she did not know what was happening around her. In spite of her misfortunes, she thought herself still fortunate: she doubted herself no more than she doubted God, and was in haste to proceed with the accomplishment of her mission" (16: 128).

Further, as such groundless confidence could not be other than perilous to her on the battlefield, her presence there often proved to be a nuisance to her superior officers. For example, the fact that "for more than three months the voices had been drumming in her ears the attack on Paris" (16: 72) caused her to persist in that attack long after its hopelessness had become apparent to the military realists in command. Ultimately they were compelled to drag her from the field by main force. "The Maid," France comments, "did not wish to leave the square. Doubtless she was listening to her saints and perceiving herself surrounded by celestial hosts" (16: 77). [17]

The voices, moreover, encouraged in her a kind of presumption which proved to be fatally perilous because it put her in direct conflict with the major sources of authority in her time. In a letter to the city of Rheims, she declared that she might refuse to honor a truce which Charles VII had recently made with the Duke of Burgundy. France comments, "What occurred to her is what necessarily occurs to everyone who imagines himself entrusted with a divine mission: that is, to constitute herself as a spiritual and temporal power transcending the powers that be and fatally opposed to them—a dangerous illusion producing those shocks in which, as a rule, the divinely illuminated are crushed" (16: 8-9).

Finally, when Joan was brought to the stake, her saints did not scruple to upbraid her for the obstinacy of her commitment. "Either you must take back what you said," they told her, "or we must abandon you to the secular arm" (16: 348). By inducing her to recant, they misled her to her doom.

Thus, France's handling of Joan's voices, in spite of his professed admiration for visionaries, tends to confirm the Naturalist claim that Romantic subjectivism cannot meet the test of experience. "Whatever our philosophical doubts may be," he wrote in 1887, "we are compelled to act in life as if we did not doubt. Seeing a beam falling upon his head, Pyrrho would have turned aside, even though he took the beam for a vain and unintelligible appearance. He would naturally enough have been afraid to receive from the blow the appearance of a crushed man."[18]

The Pyrrhonists are criticized in the article "Pyrrhonisme" in Diderot's *Encyclopedia* for failing to bring their personal conduct into line with their philosophical professions. "A man single and true," it declares, "will not have two philosophies, one for the cabinet and the other for society. He will not establish in speculation principles which he will be obliged to forget in practice." And in fact, France's historiographical practice contradicts his subjectivist theory at nearly every point. He asserts, for example, that the distinction between hallucination and objective perception has no foundation in reality, yet argues on the basis of that distinction that Sts. Catherine and Margaret did not exist. And his comments on the subject of reality and illusion remind us that the Pyrrhonists were famous for their lawyer-like eagerness to argue on both sides of any given question. On one occasion, speaking as a lover of the visionary, he claims that the inability to believe in the real existence of hallucinatory personages results entirely from a culpable want of imagination.[19] On another, speaking as a critic of autobiography, he insists that "there is in each of us a need for truth which causes us at certain moments to reject the most beautiful fictions." [20]

Clearly it is this last attitude that prevails in *Vie de Jeanne d'Arc*: France's Naturalist contention that the province of history lies in "the effort to discover the natural sequence of events" seems to have protected that work from the irrational implications of his own skeptical subjectivism. "If I excuse, if I admire, the visions of the poor little shepherd girl," he told his friend Loyson, "it does not follow that in writing her story I have given credence to the miraculous. Quite the contrary; I have continually borne in mind that the duty of the intellectual is to explain all facts by relating them to natural causes."[21] But the resultant realism is the consequences of an insuperable temperamental bent rather than of that disinterested love for truth which, following the example of Renan, he professes in his preface (15: 68).[22] When someone advised him, many years later, that the self-deception of the *voyant* can be achieved at will, he replied, "I do not have sufficient imagination. I too am a hardheaded man, magnetized by that most deceptive, most ancient, most wrinkled, and most crabbed of all illusions: the illusion of the truth. I am suspicious in the face of the supernatural. I should like to know why! But in any case, it is so. I examine, I reflect, I have the crooked fingers of the skeptic who takes things apart."[23] He betrays the relation which this destructive Skepticism bore to his temperamental melancholy in a revealing remark in his essay on Mérimée. "His sadness," he asks, "was it not rather that of the skeptic for whom the universe is only a succession of incomprehensible images, and who is equally afraid of life and of death, since neither the one nor the other possesses any meaning for him? In short, did he not experience that bitterness of mind and heart which is the inevitable chastisement of intellectual audacity, and did he not drink to the lees what Marguerite of Angoulême has aptly named "the ennui common to every well-born creature?"[24]

THREE

JOAN AS TOOL OF THE ARMAGNAC CLERGY

In religious matters, enthusiasm always begins the edifice, but astuteness completes it.
Voltaire, *Essai sur les moeurs*

Unlike Twain, France scoffs at the idea that the Maid was impelled by what he calls a "reasoned enthusiasm." "This attitude," he declares in his preface, "was not without its drawbacks. It let freethinking historians to exaggerate to the point of absurdity the intellectual faculties of this child, to make a ridiculous attribution to her of military talent, and to substitute for the naive marvel of the fifteenth century a polytechnic phenomenon. The Catholic historians of our time are in much better accord with nature and with the truth when they make the Maid a saint" (15: 33). But France's agreement with those historians is actually somewhat superficial; while they were often willing to grant that Joan's intellectual endowments were not exceptional, they concluded that her success can be explained only by supposing that she was sent of God.

The weakness in this argument, according to France, is that it rests upon the anti-Naturalist fallacy that Joan's career can best be understood in isolation from its environmental determinants. Thus, in "Sur Jeanne d'Arc," he remarks, "I believe, for my part, that in the last analysis nothing in the life of Joan of Arc escapes a rational interpretation. The mistake of her biographers is to over-isolate this young girl, to shut her up in a chapel. They ought, on the contrary, to place her within her natural group, in the midst of those prophetesses and seeresses who abounded at that time. . . [and] who, in common with Joan, had visions, revelations, and the gift of prophecy."

In the same essay, France denied that this Naturalistic approach would have the effect of discrediting Joan. "She will not appear either the less beautiful or the less great," he remarked, "for having been the embodiment of the dream of every spirit, for having been in truth the one who was expected."[1] In fact, there is no reason in logic why a

Naturalistic approach to biography need be anti-heroic. But in the age of Darwin philosophical Naturalism, like the literary naturalism it engendered, tended to be both pessimistic and fatalistic. "It has taught [man]" France observed of science in 1890, "that everything within him as around him is determined by fatal laws, that the will is an illusion, and that he is merely a machine ignorant of his own mechanism."[2] In working out his theories about the Maid in subsequent years, he not only deprived her of uniqueness but also represented her as the helpless victim of her circumstances. "When we examine more closely the *hallucinés* who believed they had a mission, we are struck by the similarity—even the identity—between their psychic states and the acts which resulted from them" (10: 513). Nine years later, in the preface to the biography, he concluded from this position that such visionaries are subject to a "déterminisme étroite":

> If we submit mystics of this type to examination, if we compare them closely the one with the other, we discern that they present among themselves traits of resemblance which we can pursue down to the minutest details—that they all repeat each other in certain of their words and in certain of their acts. And, in recognizing the strict determinism to which the movements of these *illuminés* are subjected, it may be that we shall experience some surprise at seeing the human machine function, under the action of a single mysterious agent, with this fatal uniformity. [15: 31]

"Joan," France then concludes, "belongs to this religious group. . . ." It would be difficult to imagine a claim that departed more drastically from Twain's view of her as a transcendent figure.

A serious weakness in France's theory is that it fails to identify the "mysterious agent." One remark which appears to attempt to clarify this matter actually tends to obscure it. After comparing Joan with three other seers, France observes that "the similarities which these three men, in spite of the contrast in sex, present to Joan of Arc are intimate and profound: they pertain to their nature itself; and the differences which at first sight appear to separate Joan so widely from these visionaries, are of an aesthetic, social and historical character, and are consequently exterior and contigent" (15: 32). But whatever notion of the "nature itself" of the individual as a thing separable from his sex France is here asserting, it is clearly inconsistent with any attempt to account for the Maid's behavior as a product of menstrual irregularity. And it renders equally untenable the idea that all such visionaries are afflicted with a hemi-anesthesia of the right side. How, then, can we define in Naturalist terms, the relation which France discerns between the "psychic states" of these seers and "the acts which resulted from them"? What is this "mysterious agent" that can produce, from an indeterminate number of different psychic phenomena, a "fatal uniformity"?

Some of France's pronouncements on this subject suggest that it may be nothing more "mysterious" than the influence of Catholic doctrine. In *Pierre Nozière*, for example, he makes much of the fact that, like Joan, the Breton seer Yves Nicolazic "resisted the celestial voice at first, pleading his weakness, his ignorance, and the greatness of the task" (10: 513). Yet this response is presumably just what we should expect from a Christian who is firm in the humility enjoined by his faith. Nor is there anything mysterious in another fact which France emphasizes: that visionaries of this sort commonly give a "sign" in token of their divine calling.[3] According to Catholic doctrine, God has promised to indicate by means of miracles the approval which he has granted to his faithful children.[4]

One feature which France attributes to the careers of these visionaries, however, clearly has nothing to do with such Christian notions of religious vocation. Drawing apparently upon Renan, who held that the success of all great religious movements has depended largely upon pious fraud, he claimed that seers of Joan's devotional type are invariably exploited by people who understand the political usefulness of imposing upon popular superstition. Indeed, he draws upon this hypothesis for a rather extravagant theory: that the idea for Joan's mission originated in the mind of an unknown priest in Lorraine who, in order to bring peace and harmony to his distracted church, inculcated in her the delusion that she was divinely appointed to save France. "We are brought to believe," he explains, "that she had fallen under certain influences; that is true of all visionaries: a director, who remains unseen, guides them. So it must have been in Joan's case" (15: 34).[5]

This theory is hard to reconcile with the available evidence, for Joan had insisted at Rouen that her missionary aspirations had come to her entirely from her voices. Yet it offered one very real advantage to France as a Naturalist historian: it enabled him, in conformity with his determinist conception of her, to account for her extraordinary achievement as an entirely natural effect of clerical coaching. Thus, details of her career which are commonly regarded by anti-Naturalists as evidence either of supernatural sanction or of the inspiration of genius are converted by France into arguments to support his

Naturalist thesis. One such detail concerns her idea that the Dauphin should give his kingdom to God in order to receive it back *en commende* (that is, in fief). Shaw, writing in 1923, regarded this recommendation as a clear proof of inspired moral and political originality on Joan's part. France, on the other hand, merely remarks, "It was not the people of her village who had taught her this term. She was reciting a prophecy which she had not invented and which manifestly had been constructed for her" (15: 34).[6]

Convenient as the hypothesis of clerical coaching may have been for France, however, it could not, without elaboration, provide a solution to the problems raised by Joan's career. After all, the other visionaries whom he had characterized as being of her class had also enjoyed the advantages of such coaching; yet not one of them had come close to rivaling her accomplishments. Hence, the logic of France's Naturalist position required him to assume that her success had been determined by some feature peculiar to her specific situation. Accordingly, after conceding in his preface that the other seers of her sort "failed miserably, whereas she grew in strength and flowered into legend," he added, "But it is the nature of the scientific mind to recognize alike in the loveliest and in the most abortive specimens of a given type common characteristics which indicate an identical origin" (15: 32).

In other words, the conditions which determine the measure of success enjoyed by such visionaries "are of an aesthetic, social, and historical character, and are consequently exterior and contigent."

What, then, were those conditions in her case? France seems to have believed that one of the most decisive lay in the adroitness with which she was managed. In spite of the absolute silence of his sources on that subject, he did not hesitate to attribute to the mysterious cleric whom he claims had taken charge of her "a mind skillful in governing souls, in inciting to action" (15: 122). After complaining in his preface that the ingenuity with which the Armagnac faction had set her to work had never been adequately appreciated, he insists in his text that the faction made adroit use of her "to give courage to the French, to terrify the English, and to prove to everyone that God, Milord St. Michael, and Milady St. Catherine were Armagnacs" (15: 36, 496).

Yet even the most skillful management, France apparently believed, could not have raised Joan to the eminence she ultimately attained had she not been favored by a peculiarity of Medieval politics. He explains in his account of her first interview with Charles, "It was the custom for saints to hold converse with kings, and the custom for kings to pay heed to them. How could a pious prince disdain this marvelous source of counsel? He would in so doing have provoked the censure of the most judicious" (15: 246).

That France regarded this political convention as having been decisive in securing the Maid's success is clear from an episode in *l'Orme du mail*, a novel which he had written twelve years before. That episode, since it deals with the career of just such a visionary in contemporary France, seems to have been intended to explore the question what sort of success Joan's like might be expected to enjoy in the modern world. Thus its subject, a certain Mlle. Deniseau, clearly belongs to the class of visionaries "who believed they had a mission." She, like Joan, has been visited by a messenger from the Church Triumphant; she, like Joan, has received from that source powers of clairvoyance and prophecy; and she, like Joan, has been requested by it to save her country from disaster by restoring its legitimate monarch to the throne. Moreover, she has been encouraged in these delusions by a shrewd ecclesiastic, who has fostered them in her in order to increase his prestige with the local monarchist party. Yet in spite of these resemblances to the Maid, Mlle. Deniseau never achieves a comparable recognition. To realize her goals, she, like Joan, needs the support of the local authorities, and the prefect of the district, M. Worms Clavelin, differs from Joan's Captain Baudricourt in being too much of a rationalist to take her missionary pretentions seriously. What is more, he also has too much at stake in the republican government not to be offended by her ardent loyalist propagandizing. Where Baudricourt had provided the Maid with the protection she needed to gain the ear of the king, M. Worms Clavelin actually makes a deal with the archbishop to have her modern counterpart silenced.

Mlle. Deniseau's downfall, however, can have come as no surprise to M. Bergeret, France's mouthpiece in the novel. "Nonetheless, I do not believe," he had predicted, "that her good fortune will be great or lasting. Our prefect, M. Worms Clavelin, is lacking in a certain civility, but he is less foolish than Baudricourt, and it is no longer the custom for heads of state to give audience to visionaries. M. Felix Faure will not receive from his confessor the counsel to try out Mademoisell Deniseau," (11:105).[7]

This implies that Joan owed her success neither to divine grace nor to supernatural inspiration, but merely to having been born at a time when people in power were still capable of taking visionaries seriously. In his *Vie de Jésus* Renan had adopted a similar position in discussing the prophet Elijah. "Let us imagine a hermit," he wrote, "dwelling among the byways near our capitols, emerging from them from time to time to present himself at the palaces of our sovereigns, thrusting aside the guards and, in an imperious voice, announcing to our kings the revolution of which he has been the sponsor. The very idea makes us smile. Such, nonetheless, was Elijah. Elijah the Tishbite in our time would not get past the gates of the Tuileries." For Renan, however, the failure which such seers would enjoy under modern conditions merely demonstrates the spiritual emptiness of our era. "The breath of the Lord blew freely among them," he explains; "among us it is restrained by the iron bands of a trivial society, condemned to an irremediable mediocrity." (HOC 1: 464-65). France, by contrast, appears to have perceived in the same circumstance a proof that seers and prophets are not quite sane. "Imagine a shepherd lass," he told his private secretary, "impatient to reveal to the president of the republic what the angels have revealed to her concerning France while she was watching her flocks. Our shepherdess will go first to seek her curé, who will treat her as a lunatic. Egged on by her celestial voices, she will proceed on foot to the Prefecture. She will not reach the prefect. Do you know what the fate of Joan of Arc would be nowadays, my dear lad? Prison or the madhouse—the snake pit."[8]

Thus, France's Naturalism, unlike Renan's, ultimately led him to adopt an anti-heroic approach to visionary experience. Rejecting his mentor's pantheistic conception of nature as a vehicle for "the breath of the Lord," he conceived of it rather as a congeries of blind and impersonal forces of which the visionary himself is merely another helpless victim. In this, he was the child of his age.

FOUR

JOAN AS RELIGIOUS FANATIC

> *Eventually, the superstitious man becomes fanatic, and*
> *then his zeal is capable of every crime in the name of the*
> *Lord.*
>
> Voltaire, *Homilies Pronounced at London*

When Naturalism is applied to ethics, it characteristically leads to a rejection of moral absolutism. If ethical conclusions are like those of the sciences in being derivable only from the observation of nature, then presumably they too must be subject to revision and correction. "Recognition that ethical formulations may require alteration," writes one modern Naturalist, "is a consequence of noting the pervasiveness of change."[1] And in *The Future of Science* Renan claims that morality as such, in the sense of adherence to conventional social codes, may one day be replaced by the ideal of perfecting men's natures through an increase in scientific understanding.[2]

France, evidently in reaction against his mentor's extravagant faith in science, began by rejecting the Naturalist position in ethics on essentially Pyrrhonist grounds. According to the Roman skeptic Sextus Empiricus, Pyrrho reacted to mores as he did to all other phenomena: though he questioned them, he recommended accepting them on the argument that there can be no good reason not to:

> He maintained, said Diogenes, that nothing is either honest nor dishonest, just nor unjust, and the same for everything else. That nothing exists really and in truth, but that in all things men govern themselves according to law and custom, for a thing is no more this than that.[3]

From this position France at one time drew two important tenets, neither of which is consistent with a scientific ethic: that there is no essential relation between morality and knowledge, and that virtue therefore consists entirely in conformity to convention. "Morality and science," he wrote in 1895, "are not necessarily tied to one another. Those who expect to make men better by instructing them are not very good observers of nature. They do not perceive that the sciences destroy prejudices, the foundation of mores."[4]

This, obviously, is an inherently conservative ethical stance. "We must consider," France wrote in 1888, "that Pyrrhonism is never unattended by a profound attachment to custom and usage. Now the custom of the greatest number is properly morality: it takes a skeptic to be always moral and a good citizen."[5] But inasmuch as he regards his virtues as "prejudices," even the conservatism of the skeptic cannot be very enthusiastic; and two years earlier, in an article on Jules Lemaître's novel *Sérénus*, France had argued that the habit of skepticism does in fact have the effect of paralyzing commitment.

Lemaître's protagonist, an intellectual of ancient Rome, provided France with a case in point. Invited into a Christian temple by his newly converted sister, Sérénus finds himself torn between admiration for the exalted conception of a man-god whose love transfigures the souls of his worshippers and an aristocratic contempt for the vulgarity and philistinism displayed by those worshippers. This ambivalence also appears in his response to the unquestioning faith of the Christians; for he, like the Pyrrhonists, is immobilized by his skeptical inability to exhaust all of the arguments for or against any given line of conduct or ground of belief. Hence, although he ultimately allows himself to be martyred by the followers of the new divinity, he never enjoys a true conversion: to the end his detachment from the world remains ironic rather than ascetic.[6]

France's attitude toward Sérénus's plight was clearly sympathetic, but he saw it nevertheless as the result of a diseased will. "The trouble is that one ceases to act when he is like that," he observes (6: 23). Many years later, in conversation with his friend Nicolas Segur, he remarked that great men of action such as Caesar and Napoleon have always been unreflective. "They were strong; they conquered cities—and souls. If they had possessed understanding, if they had consecrated their intelligence, not to acting, but to meditating, they too would have written a few volumes in octavo."[7]

In keeping with this view, France represents the Maid as owing the strength of her commitment, and consequently much of her effectiveness on the battlefield, to precisely the sort of uncompromising religious faith that had antagonized Sérénus. At Orleans, "she performed better than the others, not because she knew more about it; she knew less. But she had more heart. While each was thinking of himself, she alone thought of everyone: while each was holding back, she did not hold back in the slightest, having offered herself unreservedly in advance" (15: 395). Moreover, this devotion made her more decisive in action than her commanders since they, being more critical than she, were more reluctant to take unmilitary risks. They refused, for example, to attack the Tourelles (a bridgehead over the Loire at Orleans) lest the resulting depletion of their strength within the town should enable the British to force their way within the walls. But the Maid's counsel, dismissing these military scruples, ordered her to proceed boldly. "Mme. St. Catherine and Mme. St. Margaret were not afraid of anything," he observed. "To have doubts is to be afraid; they had no doubts whatever. They had not read Vegetius' *De Re Militari*. If they had read Vegetius the town would have been lost" (15: 409).

Thus, like his contemporary William James, France seems to have concluded that heroic enthusiasm is virtually impossible without some capacity for non-rational commitment. "Who gains promotions, boons, appointments," James had asked in "The Will to Believe" (1896), "but the man in whose life they are seen to play the part of live hypotheses. . .? His faith acts on the powers above him as a claim and creates its own verification."[8]

In this opinion France was once again following in his mentor's footsteps. "Reflection leads only to doubt," Renan had written in his *Vie de Jesus*; "and if the authors of the French Revolution, for instance, had had to be persuaded in advance by sufficiently lengthy meditations, they would all have arrived at old age without ever having done anything" (HOC 1:331-32). For Renan, great ideas are arrived at not by conscious ratiocination but by imagination and intuition. Hence he held of Jesus what, for similar reasons, Shaw held of Joan: that he was an inspired personage, and that the genuineness of his inspiration was guaranteed by the superiority of his values.

This approach, however, was not open to France in dealing with the Maid. Unlike Twain, he was too consistent in his Naturalism not to be aware that the Romantic doctrine of inspiration, since it premises that man subsists in a state of intimate harmony with the forces that govern his world, is logically dependent upon Romantic Pantheism. Whereas both Twain and Shaw were willing to follow Michelet's lead in regarding Joan as an inspired precursor of French nationalism, France actually argued—and precisely on Naturalist grounds—that she had been incapable of any such originality. "Certainly the daughter of Isabelle Romee," he declares in his preface, "had no more idea of the fatherland, such as we conceive it today, than she had of the landed property that is its basis; she did not imagine anything comparable to what we call 'the nation'; that is an entirely modern thing. . ." (15: 54-55).

France's hostility to the Romantic doctrine of inspiration did not rest upon its logical grounds alone. In keeping with his anti-dogmatic skepticism, he held that the Romantic rebel's faith in the infallibility of his intuitions renders him as dogmatic and intolerant as the social conservatives against whom he is rebeling. And here again it is instructive to compare his views with those of Renan. When men and women are endowed with great spiritual superiority, Renan declares, it often happens that "their persuasion that God is in them and is perpetually concerned about them is so great that they are not at all afraid of imposing on others; our reserve, our respect for the opinions of others, which is a function of our weakness, could never be appropriate to them." This being the case, however, it is necessarily difficult for ordinary men to distinguish between the man of genius and the mere intolerant fanatic who suffers from megalomania. "The madman," Renan concedes, "stands shoulder to shoulder here with the man inspired. . ." (HOC 1: 80). It may be that the only way to defend the latter from the charge of such megalomania is to suppose, as Renan did, that his conviction "that God is in him and is perpetually concerned about him" is substantially correct.

At all events, one consequence of France's rejection of the Romantic doctrine of inspiration is that his Maid appears to be suffering from delusions of grandeur. "Living and conversing all the days of her life with angels and saints, in the splendor of the Church Triumphant," France declares at one point, "this young peasant girl believed that in her were all force and all prudence, all wisdom and all counsel" (16: 9). Ironically, the habit of skepticism which alone might have served as a corrective to such delusions was actually forbidden to Joan by her religious faith.

Nor, in France's view, was this extravagant self-conceit the only unfortunate consequence of her incapacity for skepticism. It rendered her uncritical not merely of herself but of anyone clever enough to take advantage of her vague religious enthusiasm. In fact, he discovered evidence of this shortcoming in her desire to conduct a crusade against the Hussites. Since this project had nothing to do with her crusade against the English, he did not hesitate to attribute it to "the mendicant monks who had charge of her"; and he suggested that in their attempts to inspire her with it they were aided by her total inability to rise above the commonplace religious prejudices of her time. "She thought of these Bohemian heretics what all the world thought," he declared. In words which ironically recall Mark Twain's description of her as "a mirror in which the lowly hosts of France were clearly reflected," he added, "she had the soul of the multitudes; her opinions were made of the opinions of all" (16: 121-22).

No passage in France's text reveals more clearly than this one the way in which his anti-heroic approach to Joan of Arc's biography had been shaped by the conspiracy against Dreyfus. To France that young Jewish officer had fallen victim to precisely the sort of mindless religious intolerance which he here attributes to the Maid. In speaking of the unjust accusation lodged against Pyrot, the character who represents Dreyfus in *Penguin Island* (1908), he remarks, "it was not doubted, because the thing was repeated everywhere, and in the public mind, to repeat is to prove. It was not doubted because people desired that Pyrot be guilty, and one believes what one desires; and because, after all, the faculty for doubt is rare among men: very few minds carry its seeds, which are not developed without cultivation" (18: 259). Considering the emphasis which this passage places on the moral necessity for doubt, "Pyrot" appears to be appropriately named.[9] The Dreyfus affair had taught France that the skeptic has a vitally important social duty to fulfill and that, far from committing one to conformism, that duty requires the constant questioning of current ethical judgments.

After 1897, then, it became increasingly difficult for France to believe in the moral necessity for "prejudices." One surmises that this change of heart must very soon have begun to affect his attitude toward the Maid; by 1900 he was attacking the mindless fanaticism of the anti-Dreyfusards in language which bears an obvious pertinence to her anti-Hussite intolerance. "The most detestable thing about ignorance," he declared, "is that it nourishes those prejudices which prevent us from performing our true functions while imposing false ones on us that are painful and sometimes pernicious and cruel—until we see the best-natured people, under the sway of ignorance, become criminal out of duty." After adding that the history of religion provides us with innumerable examples of such destructive ignorance, he repudiated his previous position that there is no essential relation between morality and knowledge:

> If we reflect upon the miseries which, from the age of the cavemen until our still barbarous times, have overwhelmed unhappy humanity, we almost always discover their cause in a false interpre-

tation of the phenomena of nature and in one or another of those theological doctrines which afford a stupid and atrocious explication to the universe. Bad physics leads to bad ethics; and that is enough so that for centuries generations of men have passed from birth to death in an abyss of suffering and of desolation.[10]

Clearly at that rate there is much to be said in favor of the Naturalist position in ethics. And indeed, whatever France may have claimed to the contrary, he seems to have realized even before the Dreyfus affair that the moral life is inescapably dependent upon moral intelligence. As early as 1892, responding to the claim of a Catholic irrationalist that the first duty of man is to sacrifice intellect in the interest of faith, France declared "Tolerance is so precious in my opinion that I do not think it is too dearly paid for at the cost of the sweetest creeds," adding, "God forbid that I should prefer anything to goodness. But we must be intelligent in order to be good; we must understand in order to love."[11]

FIVE

JOAN AS MARTYR TO SUPERSTITION

*In these matters I fear this: that you perhaps may think you
are beginning an impious study and entering upon an evil path.
But on the contrary: Religion herself has more often been the
cause of evil and impious acts. For example, at Aulis the chosen
leaders of the Greeks–the foremost of men–foully defiled the
altar of virgin Diana with the blood of Iphianassa. . . . So great
are the evils to which Religion has been able to persuade.*
Lucretius, *De Rerum Natura*, bk. 1

France seems to have discovered virtually the whole value of Joan's
commitment in the pathos of her martyrdom. In his preface, after
remarking that she sacrificed her life to restore the Dauphin to the
throne of his fathers, he added, "It was thus that she survived her
cause. The highest enterprises perish in their defeat, and more certainly still in their victory. The devotion that inspires them endures as
a deathless example. . . . Cities, empires, republics rest upon sacrifice" (15: 35).

Behind this pronouncement lies a theory of the moral value of
suffering which France had presented in 1887 in the article "Virtue in
France." "An exalted philosophy," he asserted, "will not bemoan the
immortality of universal evil. It will recognize, on the contrary, that
evil is necessary and that it ought to endure, for without it man would
not have a thing to do in this world." Nature, he concedes, imposes
savagery on man, who must kill in order to live; but he is redeemed by
suffering, which educates him in such natural virtues as courage,
patience, and benevolence.

This last idea he attributes to a philosophical angel—a creature who
possesses that Olympian detachment which Voltaire enjoins on the
scientific student of man. Though blessed with a celestial remoteness
from human affairs, this person, unlike most heavenly beings, seems
not to have been endowed with a compensating religious enthusiasm.
The species to which he belongs neither sings nor adores but observes. In examining our actions, France explains, he will at first be

horrified by "the large number of crimes which hunger and love ceaselessly bring to birth among us." In time, however, he will discover that we are suffering, and "all our grandeur will be revealed to him."

> Then you will hear him murmur, "They are born infirm, anguished, starved, destined to devour each other. And not all of them do devour each other. I perceive some who, though in great distress, stretch out their arms to one another. . . . The earth is evil: it is insensible. But man is good since he suffers."
> [6: 298-99] [1]

Here again France's position appears to be anti-Naturalist. If values are to be derived from nature, they must presumably be defined in terms of what men naturally desire. "Virtue," Voltaire asserts, "is the habit of doing things which are pleasing to men and vice the habit of doing those things which are displeasing to them."[2] In his "Antinaturalism in Extremis," the American Naturalist John Dewey includes an attack on Christian asceticism as part of his critique of Christian supernaturalism in ethics. Quoting Cardinal Newman, Dewey complains that, according to Catholic orthodoxy, " 'The pattern man, the just, the upright, the generous, the honorable, the conscientious, if he is all this not from a supernatural power, but from *mere natural virtue*,' has the prospect of heaven 'closed and refused to him.' When such measure is meted out to virtues like honor, uprightness, justice, and generosity, one readily gathers how conduct proceeding from appetite and desire will be judged. For the latter are deeply dyed with the Pauline and Augustinian view of the total corruption of the body and lusts of carnal flesh."[3]

France's position, on the other hand, appears to be in conformity with Christian doctrine—indeed he sometimes quotes the New Testament in support of it. "Humanity has an obscure consciousness of the necessity for suffering." he declares in "Virtue in France." "It has included pious sadness among the virtues of its saints. Blessed be they that mourn, and cursed be the fortunate. For having raised this cry the Gospels have reigned for two thousand years upon the earth" (6: 297).

France's argument that virtue cannot exist without suffering derives from a classic Christian solution to the problem of evil. According to Bayle, Lactantius adopted it in his *De ira dei*. But, Bayle also points out, the argument is heretical in its implications, since it would deny such virtues to all those in supernal bliss, including not only the unfallen Adam but the saints and angels in paradise, and even God Himself.[4]

Here again, then, France's apparent agreement with Christian orthodoxy appears upon closer scrutiny to be misleading. The ascetic
embraces suffering largely as an expression of contempt for the vain
delights of this world. France, on the other hand, valued it solely as a
means of growing in "mere natural virtue." To the ascetic position as
such he was no more sympathetic than Dewey. In fact, he concurred
with Dewey in perceiving it as a device on the part of the Church to
secure its moral authority over its members. "A long religious tradition, which still weighs heavy upon us," he told an audience of
laborers in 1889, "teaches us that privation, suffering and sorrow are
desirable, and that there are special merits attached to voluntary
self-denial. What an imposture! It is by telling people that they must
suffer in this world in order to be happy in the other that they have
obtained from them an abject resignation to all oppressions and to all
iniquities. Let us not listen to the priests who teach us that suffering is
excellent. It is joy that is good."[5]

Finally, since he believed that all life will ultimately become extinct,
France insisted that virtue is ultimately futile. In place of the Christian
view which enjoins sacrifice because it is pleasing to God, he advanced the peculiarly modern view that the justification for all commitment is to be found in its very futility. Pointing out in "Virtue in
France" that "the object of the most beautiful sacrifices is often trivial
and sometimes worthless," he comments, "Self-dedication and
heroism are like great works of art: they have no end but themselves. It
could almost be said that their uselessness is the ground of their
greatness. One devotes oneself for the sake of devoting oneself"
(6:296).

From a Naturalist point of view this remark too would appear to be
unsatisfying. Naturalism, even when not Epicurean, is normally
utilitarian. In his *Traité de métaphysique* Voltaire remarks, "Virtue and
vice, moral good and moral evil, are. . . in every country, that which
is useful or harmful to society."[6] By insisting that all virtues, including
that of self-sacrifice, are ultimately dependent upon suffering, France
was actually confirming the Naturalist point which Voltaire had
made: that valid ethical knowledge can proceed only from a direct
awareness of human moral experience.[7] And as was the case with
Voltaire, this perception lies at the heart of his hostility to Christian
supernaturalism in ethics. In common with most utilitarians, Voltaire
and France held that the Church, by making its moral doctrine depend
upon revelation, had alienated its conception of virtue from the immediate needs of mankind.[8]

And yet, France reasoned, precisely because He cannot suffer, the Christian God cannot be virtuous. In his *Apology for Raymond Sebond,* Montaigne had argued that, as a means of humbling the moral and intellectual pride of man, God's transcendence alienates him from natural virtue as well as from natural curiosity. "What has He to do with reason and intelligence," Montaigne asks, "which we use to arrive at apparent things from things obscure, seeing that there is nothing obscure to God? . . . Fortitude in bearing pain, toil, and dangers, appertains to him as little, since these three things have no access to him."[9] France subtly inverts this argument in order to exalt the humanist pride of man at God's expense: "It is through suffering," remarks his newly-fallen Satan, "that, making a first experience of nature, we are compelled to understand and overcome her. When she obeys we will be as gods. But even were she forever to conceal from us her mysteries, to refuse us arms, and to keep the secret of the lightning, we ought still to congratulate ourselves on having known suffering, since it reveals to us new sentiments, sweeter and more precious than all those experienced in eternal beatitude, and since it inspires us with love and pity, which are unknown to heaven."[10]

We might expect with these views that France's account of the Maid's passion would be somewhat heterodox—and in fact his Joan falls short, in a number of ways, of being a true Christian martyr. First, the Church, does not accept his idea that the merit of a given sacrifice is not dependent on its object: it requires specifically that the martyr's death be incurred either in defense of Christian virtue or in witness to the faith. [11] The claim that the Maid had given her life merely to restore the Dauphin to his heritage was actually urged against her by the Devil's Advocate in the trial that led to her canonization.

Furthermore, in identifying its martyrs, the Church considers not only their motives but those of their executioners: death, it insists, must be inflicted *in odium fidei.* Here again France's Naturalism led him to assume an anti-orthodox position. The obvious Naturalist objection to any ethic which encourages indifference to suffering is that it may induce one to inflict suffering unnecessarily.[12] "Faith is the mainspring of hatred as well as love," France once declared.[13] Whereas Joan's Catholic apologists have usually regarded her judges as cynical and anti-religious hypocrites, France, by contrast, represents them as being conscientious victims of vicious Catholic superstitions. "The Rouen chapter," he remarked in the preface, "lacked neither courage nor independence. . . they believed, most of them, that they were proceeding truthfully in a matter of faith. . . . Many of them doubtless imagined that by their sentence they were maintaining, against the inciters of schism and heresy, the orthodoxy of the Catholic faith and the unity of Catholic obedience; they wanted to judge well" (15: 47). In the text, with characteristic irony, he observes, "As they were very learned, they perceived magicians and sorcerers where others would not have suspected them. They opined that doubt concerning the power of demons over men and things was not only heresy and impiety, but also subversion of all society both natural and political. Each of the doctors seated there in the chapel of the castle had burned ten, twenty, fifty witches, all of whom had confessed. Would it not have been foolish, in the light of that fact, to doubt the existence of witches?" (16: 241-42).

But it was with respect to the canonical requirements that death be incurred voluntarily that Joan's short-comings as a martyr were most gravely conspicuous. The Church recognizes, of course, that the fear of death and the desire to avoid suffering are natural human emotions. It also holds, however, that in the martyr's case they are controlled by another emotion which transcends the merely natural, namely, an exalted love of God. Consequently, it regards martyrdom as the highest expression of the virtue of fortitude. France's Joan proved, in the hour of trial, to be seriously lacking in that virtue. When the rescue promised her by her voices failed to materialize, then, "feeling both heaven and earth forsake her, she fell into a deep despair" (16: 367). Although France concedes that her consoling hallucinations may have returned to her on the road to the stake, he adds, "It appears nevertheless that she was broken, and that nothing held fast in her but an infinite horror of death and the piety of a child" (16: 379).

Thus, whatever France may say about it in his preface, he has actually represented Joan's martyrdom not as the exalted self-sacrifice of a heroically virtuous saint but as the merely pathetic ordeal of a bewildered and helpless victim of superstitious delusions. His claim that by undergoing that ordeal she had set a noble example of devotion is further undermined by his insistence that she was as intolerant as her judges and would have been equally unmerciful in their place. "We are struck with pity at this depressing spectacle," he remarks, "and we experience a feeling of distress in reflecting that while she is threatening with extermination the disciples of that John Huss who has been treacherously bound over and burned as a heretic, she is herself on the point of being sold to her enemies and condemned to the stake as a sorceress" (16: 126).

France in 1889, in an article on Rabelais, remarked, "I should accuse martyrs of a measure of fanaticism. I suspect between them and their executioners a certain natural affinity and I fancy that they become executioners with pleasure the moment they get enough power." In the same place he made explicit how much he preferred the tolerant skepticism of such detached intellectuals as Sérénus to the inflexible dogmatism of Christian fanatics like Joan:

> We must leave martyrdom to those who, not knowing how to doubt, possess in their very simplicity the excuse for their stubbornness. There is a measure of impertinence in getting burned for an idea. With the Sérénus of M. Jules Lemaître, we are annoyed that people can be so convinced of certain things when we ourselves have sought so hard without finding, and have ended by resting content with doubt. Martyrs are wanting in irony, and that is an unpardonable fault; for without irony the world would be like a forest without birds. [7: 43]

In short, France was both too tolerant and too skeptical to adopt the Romantic cult of the hero. The only protagonist in his novels who dies for a cause—Evariste Gamelin of *The Gods Are Athirst*—is a homicidal fanatic.

SIX

HOW HISTORY IS MADE

La nature est muette, on l'interroge en vain;
On a besoin d'un Dieu qui parle au genre humain.
Voltaire, *Poème sur le désastre de Lisbonne*

In the late eighties, France argued that Joan of Arc's success should be regarded naturalistically as an expression of the medieval belief in the special virtue of the saints. At that time he denied that he had any iconoclastic intention; indeed, he spoke of her in glowing terms as "the living poetry of that sweet France which she loved with a miraculous love."[1] In the end, however, his Naturalism undermined this idealized conception by making him subtly contemptuous of the very superstitions whose poetic attractiveness he had begun by admiring. "It must be great, the power of the Holy Ghost," he told his friend Marcel le Goff, "to inspire so stupid a girl. That's the way of it. The Holy Ghost does not inspire intelligent people."[2]

What is more, this disparaging conclusion led to others more disparaging still. In the light of such incapacity, Joan's spectacular success could be plausibly explained only by supposing that she had been cleverly stagemanaged by men who understood the nature of her influence more clearly than she did. And whatever may be said of the Maid, France was too worldly wise to believe that the motives of her exploiters had been entirely patriotic and disinterested. To his friend Michel Corday he remarked, "They diverted her from taking towns which had already been destroyed, pillaged, and depopulated, and which the time to take over would be after the English occupation had restored and enriched them. So they turned their mascot instead towards Sens and Auxerres, rich cities. That, you see, is how history is made."[3]

Thus *Vie de Jeanne d'Arc*, though originally conceived as a celebration of the creative power of myth, ultimately became a savage attack on the pernicious influence of popular religious credulity. Yet France, in common with many of his contemporaries, was afflicted with a frustrated longing for faith. "It is the strength and the virtue of religions," he wrote in *Le Jardin d'Epicure*, "to teach man his reason for being and his ultimate ends. When we have repudiated the dogmas of ethical theology, as almost all of us have in this age of science and of intellectual freedom, there is no longer any way of knowing why we are in the world or what we have come there to do. Under these circumstances, he added, "we must really avoid thinking altogether in order not to become cruelly aware of the tragic absurdity of life." And he complained bitterly that "in a world in which all the light of faith has been extinguished, evil and suffering lose their very meaning and appear only as odious practical jokes and sinister farces" (9: 424-25).

Clearly, then, one of the most urgent needs of the modern world must be to find a new and viable religion. But where, in "this age of science and of intellectual freedom," is such a religion to be found? Presumably not in any return to Christian supernaturalism. "The trouble with revealed religions," France declared in 1905, "is that the revelations on which they are based represent an outmoded condition of science and of civilization."[4] Yet Naturalism can provide a religion only if the answers to the questions "why we are in the world and what we have come there to do" are objectively discoverable in nature. And how, without abandoning scientific skepticism in the interests of our emotional needs, can we presume to justify that supposition?

For a while, France apparently thought he had found answers to these questions in secular humanism—specifically in the ideal of a socialist world federation: an ideal to which, as it happens, he gave eloquent expression in the preface to *Vie de Jeanne d'Arc*. "I believe in the future union of the nations," he declared, "and I call for it on behalf of that ardent charity for the human race which, formed in the Latin consciousness in the time of Epictetus and Seneca, and extinguished for so many centuries by European barbarism, has been kindled anew in the most enlightened hearts of modern times. It is useless to tell me that these are the illusions of dream and of longing. It is longing that creates life, and the future will take pains to realize the dreams of philosophers" (15: 61). But ironically, faith failed in this case to "create its own verification." The dream in question was soon to dissolve in the savage bickering which convulsed the Left after the Great War; and this defeat of "the will to believe" doubtless accounts for much of that misanthropic despair which darkened the final years of France's life.

Thus France was unable, either in his life or in his work, to supply a positive creed which could adequately substitute for the Maid's misguided Christianity. This failure appears all the more poignant in the light of his long-standing conviction that the gradual decline of Christian faith had been a principal cause of the peculiar despair of modern times. In 1889, in an essay significantly called "Why Are We Sad?" he bemoaned the fact that science, by enlarging and correcting man's conception of the universe, had deprived him of his belief in his special dignity and of his sense of belonging to a cosmic moral order. "We have eaten of the fruits of the tree of knowledge," he complained, "and a taste of ashes has remained in our mouths." After remarking that the collapse of the old moral sanctions had greatly increased the ferocity of the social struggle for survival, he concluded:

> Along with faith and hope, we have lost charity; the three virtues which, like three ships bearing at the prow the image of a heavenly virgin, once carried destitute souls over the ocean of the world, have foundered in the same tempest. Who will bring to us a new faith? a new hope? a new charity?[5]

PART III

BERNARD SHAW & THE MAID
A Vitalist View

We have nothing to do in this world except to resign our-
selves. But noble natures understand how to give to resignation
the beautiful name of contentment. Great souls resign them-
selves with a holy joy. In the bitterness of doubt, at the midst of
universal evil, under the empty sky, they know how to keep
intact the antique virtues of the faithful. They believe, they
insist on believing. Charity for the human race enflames them.
But that is not all. They piously preserve that virtue–hope–
which Christian theology in its wisdom placed at the head of all
others because it either presupposes or replaces them. Let us
hope, then, not in humanity which, in spite of exalted efforts,
has not destroyed the evil in this world, but in those inconceiva-
ble beings who shall evolve some day from man as man has
evolved from the beast. Let us salute those geniuses of the
future. Let us rest our hopes on that universal anguish whose
transformation is the law of matter. That fruitful anguish–we
feel it burgeoning in us; it causes us to march toward an end both
inevitable and divine.

France, *Le Jardin d'Epicure*

ONE

SHAW AND VITALISM

*The moral government of God over the world is
exercized through us, who are his ministers and
persons, and a government of this description is the
only one which can be observed as practically
influencing men's conduct. God helps those who help
themselves because in helping themselves they are
helping him.*
Samuel Butler, *"God the Known and God the Unknown"*

*There are many scapegoats for our sins but the most
popular is Prov.*
Twain, Notebook 32

Although Shaw's *Saint Joan*[1] was not written until 1923, his interest
in religious heroism actually dates from a much earlier period. Twenty
years before, in complaining of the irreligiousness of Shakespeare and
Dickens, he remarked in the preface to *Man and Superman* that "they
are anarchical, and cannot balance their exposures of Angelo and
Dogberry, Sir Leicester Dedlock and Mr. Tite Barnacle, with any
portrait of a prophet or a worthy leader. . . ." He argued that, unlike
John Bunyan, who had "achieved virtue and courage by identifying
himself with the purpose of the world as he understood it," Shakespeare in particular was too much of a skeptic to succeed in endowing
his characters with that capacity for devotion to a transcendent objective which true heroism implies (3: 508-10).

Shaw apparently developed this view of the dependence of heroic
commitment upon religious conviction in reaction against the biological determinism of the followers of Darwin. The most objectionable
feature of Darwinism, he believed, was precisely that it was anti-
teleological: by representing evolution as the product of essentially
blind and impersonal natural forces it had, in Samuel Butler's phrase,
"banished mind from the universe."[2] And in the process it had
deprived men of that sense of metaphysical purpose which alone can
nerve them to heroic undertakings. "Most of the natural selection men

of the nineteenth century," Shaw declared in 1911, "were very brilliant, but they were cowards. We want to get back to men with some
belief in the purpose of the universe, with determination to identify
themselves with it and with the courage that comes from that."[3]

Darwinism was not only irreligious, as Shaw perceived it, it was
also fundamentally immoral, because its identification of competition
as the sole source of evolutionary development tended to encourage
the competitive spirit of capitalism at the expense of ethical idealism.
"The theory of the survival of the fittest," he complained in 1912,
"made the competitive system positively scientific."[4] Nine years
later, after the moral bankruptcy of that system had been glaringly
exposed by the eruption of the most terrible war in history, he declared of Darwin's doctrine in the preface to *Back to Methuselah*, "If it
be no blasphemy, but a truth of science, then the stars of heaven, the
showers and dew, the winter and summer, the fire and heat, the
mountains and hills, may no longer be called to exalt the Lord with us
by praise: their work is to modify all things by blindly starving and
murdering everything that is not lucky enough to survive in the
universal struggle for hogwash" (3: xlii-iii).

Fortunately, Shaw argued, there are a number of excellent reasons
for believing that Darwin's theory is not "a truth of science." And of
these one of the best is the plain fact that many otherwise promising
members of our species are subject to an "appetite for evolution" that
is so far from being consistent with their will to survive that it often
brings them to an early and violent end. The very existence of such an
appetite, Shaw reasoned, is inexplicable in Darwinist terms—indeed,
in any terms whatever that are not frankly metaphysical. Being neither
material nor personal, it testifies to the pressure upon the psyche of
forces that are both immaterial and superpersonal.[5] It is apparently
just this conviction that accounts for Shaw's interest in St. Joan; the
reason for regarding her as a saint, he believed, is precisely that she
herself was an embodiment of those immaterial forces.

Consequently, his characterization of her is imbued throughout by
a conception of the essentially irrational, and therefore miraculous,
character of heroic commitment. In the first scene, when Baudricourt
asks whether he really believes that she can perform miracles,
Poulengy responds, "I think the girl herself is a bit of a miracle." And
he apparently reveals what he means by this remark when, shortly
thereafter, he declares that "her words and her ardent faith in God
have put fire into me." For the most impressive feature of Joan's
character here lies in the obvious sincerity of her conviction that she is

the agent of a divine purpose —a conviction which accounts not only for the "positiveness" with which she intimidates Baudricourt's steward, and the persuasiveness with which she wins over Baudricourt, but also, and most importantly, for the courage with which she faces the prospect of battle with the formidable goddams (2: 326-27).

But however much of a "miracle" Shaw's Joan may be, she never succeeds in performing one, a fact which points up a fundamental difference between her conception of the God she is serving and that of her creator. God, as Shaw conceived him, is not a transcendent Being, capable of interfering in the orderly processes of nature. "What you have got to understand," he told a Christian audience in 1907, "is that somehow or other there is at the back of the universe a will, a life-force. You cannot think of him as a person, you have to think of him as a great purpose, a great will, and, furthermore, you have to think of him as engaged in a continual struggle to produce something higher and higher, to create organs to carry out his purpose; as wanting hands, and saying, 'I must create something with hands'; arriving at that very slowly, after innumerable experiments and innumerable mistakes, because this power must be proceeding as we proceed, because if there were any other way it would put us in that way. . . ."

Thus Shaw's "God," so far from being capable of interfering with nature on behalf of his creatures, is completely dependent on them. "It is not an omnipotent power that can do things without us," Shaw remarked of the Life Force in 1912; "it has created us in order that we might do its work. In fact, that is the way it does its work—through us."[6] Accordingly, he completely rejected the Christian conception of the miraculous, arguing that irregularities in the orderly operation of natural law can only tend to the defeat of all natural foresight. He believed devoutly that nothing was impossible for the Life Force (hence his fondness for the expression "where there's a will there's a way"), but he held just as devoutly that events which are neither Vitalist in origin nor rationally explicable must end by undermining our confidence in the sovereignty of the will over nature, and thus by subverting all meaningful religious faith.[7]

In short, Shaw objected to Christian supernaturalism, not because it is credulous but because it is irreligious. "I think a man who is not Christian enough," he wrote in 1908, "to feel that conjuror's miracles are, on the part of a god, just what cheating at cards is on the part of a man. . .is not Christian at all."[8] This idea clearly influenced his attitude toward the Maid. In the cathedral scene he allows Dunois to reproach her for relying too much upon such divine "cheating." "If you are worthy of it," he declares, "he will sometimes snatch you out of the jaws of death and set you on your feet again; but that is all: once on your feet you must fight with all your strength and all your craft. For he has to be fair to your enemy too; don't forget that." Shortly thereafter he adds, "I tell you that your little hour of miracles is over, and that from this time on he who plays the war game best will win—if the luck is on his side" (2: 377-78).

Moreover, Shaw had a more serious objection to Christian supernaturalism than that it tends to inspire such presumption. He also reasoned that it must have the effect of encouraging spiritual irresponsibility since as long as men are given to understand that they must depend for the welfare of their souls upon forces external to, and incalculable by, themselves, they cannot justifiably be held accountable for their own salvation. From this position he argued that the only sort of god whose nature is consistent with the fullest responsibility on the part of its worshipers is one who, like the Life Force, "possesses no executive powers of its own." Thus, in "The Religion of the British Empire," after asserting that he believed God, "in the popular acceptance of the word, to be completely powerless," he went on to repudiate the whole Christian ideal of resignation:

> If you don't do his work it won't be done: if you turn away from it, if you sit down and say, "Thy will be done," you might as well be the most irreligious person on the face of the earth. But if you will stand by your God, if you will say, "My business is to do your will, my hands are your hands, my tongue is your tongue, my brain is your brain, I am here to do thy work, and I will do it," you will get rid of otherworldliness, you will get rid of all that religion which is made an excuse and a cloak for doing nothing."[9]

Hence Shaw, in his play, rejected the Catholic view that Joan was endowed with supernatural powers, representing it in one of the work's most famous lines as the product of a medieval will to believe.[10] In spite of the sympathy which he professes for the idea of miracles, he ended by explaining many of the miracles which have been attributed to his heroine as the results of an entirely natural exercise of her private judgment. After all, he seems to have reasoned, when every concession has been made to the truth that Man, far from being a mere machine, is "the Temple of the Holy Ghost," the fact remains that "it is only through his own brain and hand that this Holy Ghost . . . can help him in any way."[11]

TWO

JOAN AS GALTONIC VISUALIZER

I have found again and again in my professional work that the images and ideas that dreams contain cannot possibly be explained solely in terms of memory. They have expressed new thoughts that have never yet reached the threshold of consciousness.

Jung, *Man and His Symbols*

Shaw is wrong when he claims in his preface that the nineteenth century concluded from Joan's voices that she was "mentally defective" (2: 275). On the contrary, the modern cult of the Maid coincides with the emergence of the Romantic idea that the imagination is a principal source for our knowledge of reality. Yet Shaw, unlike such Romantic admirers of Sts. Catherine and Margaret as Michelet, rests his case for them largely on the unromantic claim that they gave Joan sound practical advice. Much of his discussion of the subject in his preface is devoted to an attempt to establish that claim on the basis of a scientific psychology.

In this attempt Shaw apparently relied heavily on the work of the English naturalist Sir Francis Galton. In his *Inquiries into Human Faculty and Its Development*, Galton asserts that there are a great many mentally healthy people whose visualizing faculty is so acute that it produces hallucinations, and that their failure to realize that they are hallucinating is not always evidence they are insane. He points out that highly imaginative children are often unable to distinguish between "the real and the visionary world"; whether they ever learn to do so often depends on the nature of their upbringing rather than on their mental and emotional stability. According to him, if such a child is raised among rationalists who regard his fancies as symptoms of mental disturbance, he will naturally take pains to identify and repress them; whereas, if he grows up in a climate of opinion which is favorable to super-naturalism, he will probably develop into a full-fledged seer. Under such conditions, Galton explains, "the faintly perceived fantasies of ordinary persons become invested by the authority of reverend men with a claim to serious regard, and they increase in definition by being habitually dwelt upon."[1]

In this manner, then, the Maid's hallucinations may be accounted for merely by observing that she was born at a time when visionaries were encouraged, that her own visualizing faculty was very keen, and that her imagination had been deeply impressed by Christian iconography.[2] "If Joan was mad," Shaw reasons in his preface, "all Christendom was mad too; for people who believe devoutly in the existence of celestial personages are every whit as mad in that sense as the people who think they see them" (2: 276).

How voices and visions may become vehicles of useful information, however, remains to be determined. Galton, among many case studies, cites none in which this was true, but he does suggest one means by which such a phenomenon may be explained. Distinguishing between hallucinations, which he calls "appearances wholly due to fancy," and illusions, which are "fanciful perceptions of objects actually seen," he remarks that "there is also a hybrid case which depends on fanciful visions fancifully perceived." He adds, "It is probable that much of what passes for hallucination proper belongs in reality to the hybrid case." Thus an "induced visual cloud or blur"—that is, one which has not been produced by an external impression—may be transformed by the imagination into what Galton calls a "fancy picture." When this phenomenon occurs in the case of an "illusion" such as that of a face seen in the fire, "this fancy picture is then dwelt upon; all that is incongruous with it becomes disregarded; while all deficiencies are supplied by the fantasy,"[3] From this it can easily be seen how the mind may come unconsciously to exercise control over the objects of the visualizing faculty:

> Joan. . . . [*The cathedral clock chimes the quarter*] Hark! [*She becomes rapt*]: Do you hear? "Dear-child-of-God": just what you said. At the half-hour they will say "Be-brave-go-on." At the three-quarters they will say "I-am-thy-Help." But it is at the hour, when the great bell goes after "God-will-save-France": it is then that St Margaret and St Catherine and sometimes even the blessed Michael will say things that I cannot tell before-hand. Then, oh then—
> Dunois [*interrupting her kindly but not sympathetically*]: Then, Joan, we shall hear whatever we fancy in the booming of the bell. [2: 372-73]

Thus, according to Shaw, "Joan must be judged a sane woman in spite of her voices because they never gave her any advice that might not have come to her from her mother wit exactly as gravitation came to Newton" (2: 274).

Shaw seems, however, not to have been wholly satisfied with this prosaic explanation. After rejecting as "too vapidly commonplace" what he describes as the nineteenth-century account of Joan's voices, he asserts that the twentieth century "demands something more mystic," and adds, "I think the twentieth century is right, because an explanation which amounts to Joan being mentally defective instead of, as she obviously was, mentally excessive, will not wash" (2: 275). But in that case a major problem of the psychologist must be to determine how an illiterate country girl may come to be "mentally excessive" in the first place. It is easy to say that the "wisdom" of Joan's voices was "all Joan's own": the real problem, as Twain saw, lies in determining where she got that wisdom. Here Shaw could get no help from "modern investigators of human faculty" (2: 279-80). Galton does say that "the number of great men who have been once, twice, or more frequently subject to hallucinations is considerable" (p. 175). But he does not claim that their visions provided them with brilliant insights, much less explain the means by which such a phenomenon may occur. What was needed for that purpose, as Shaw perceived, was a theory of the creative process which would account for voices and visions as potential vehicles for inspiration. In providing such a theory he seems to have relied not on Galton's case studies but on his own researches into evolutionary biology.

The key to his rather complicated theory of Vitalist inspiration is found in his account of the traditional conception of Satan. "It was a conception of enormous value," he told an audience of heretics in 1911, "for the devil was always represented as a person who could do nothing by himself, an l that he had to tempt people to do wrong." He explained that in this respect Satan resembles the God of Vitalism, who, being similarly powerless to compel his agents, had also hit upon the device of tempting them in order to get them to fulfill his purposes. "If we conceive of God as working in that way," he added, "and having a tremendous struggle with a great, whirling mass of matter, civilization means our molding this mass to our own purposes and will, and in doing that really molding it to the will of God."[4]

What gives this conception its "enormous value," then, is that it provides an answer to the question how "a bodiless, impotent force, having no executive power of its own" can nevertheless get its work done in the world. "Temptation and inspiration mean the same thing," Shaw declared in this connection, "exactly as firmness and obstinacy mean the same thing, only people use the one word when they want to be complimentary and the other when they want to be abusive."[5] The hallucinatory character of Satan was also of service here because it indicated a precise psychological means by which organisms may be "tempted" to strive for conditions which do not yet exist, and thus pointed to a solution to the very difficult problem of identifying the origin of variation in species.

How serious a problem this was in terms of the evolutionary theory of the day is revealed by an examination of the sources of Shavian Vitalism. Samuel Butler, in *Evolution Old and New*, had urged as part of his attack on Darwin the objection that "natural selection cannot be considered a cause of variation. . .for the variations must make their appearance before they can be selected." "Suppose that it is an advantage to a horse," Butler explains, "to have an especially hard and broad hoof, then a horse born with such a hoof will indeed probably survive in the struggle for existence, but he was not born with the larger and harder hoof *because of his subsequently surviving. . . .* The variation must arise first and be preserved afterwards."[6] Yet as cogent as this objection must have seemed at the time, Butler was aware that in this matter he was no better off than Darwin. His theory of the hereditary transmission of "unconscious memory" will indeed account for the preservation of acquired faculties, but it will not explain how such faculties come to be acquired in the first place. "We can no more have an action than a creative effort of the imagination cut off from memory," he declares;[7] but how in that case can an organism learn to do anything which was not already done by its ancestors? Shaw was later to present this conundrum in terms of the Eden myth:[8] women know how to give birth because they are daughters of Eve; but how did Eve herself know?

Moreover, Henri Bergson, whose influence on Shaw's Vitalist ideas was second only to Butler's, was struck by the same difficulty. He urges it in support of his irrationalist attack upon the intellect:

> It is of the essence of reasoning to shut us up in the circle of the given. . . . If we had never seen a man swim, we might say that swimming is an impossible thing, inasmuch as, to learn to swim, we must begin by holding ourselves up in the water and, consequently, already know how to swim.

For Bergson it is "action" which enables us "to cut the knot which reasoning has tied" in this case. He explains, "But if, quite simply, I throw myself into the water without fear, I may keep myself up well enough at first by merely struggling, and gradually adapt myself to the new environment. . . ."[9] But Shaw reasoned, in effect, that there is more to such action than is implied by Bergson's description. Before one throws himself into the water, he must want to learn to swim. And as motivation is by definition a goal-directed function, he must begin by imagining something which does not yet exist, namely, himself as a swimmer.[10] Hence Bergson's solution really begs the question; although we may have no difficulty imagining ourselves swimming if we have already seen someone doing it, this condition is obviously not met by the original swimmer. Is Butler wrong, then, when he claims that we cannot have "a creative effort of the imagination cut off from memory"?

Shaw apparently found the answer in his experience as a playwright. In a letter to the *New York Times,* June 2, 1912, he replied to a request to identify "the principles which govern the dramatist":

> I am not governed by principles; I am inspired, how or why I cannot explain, because I do not know; but inspiration it must be; for it comes to me without any reference to my own ends or interests.
>
> I find myself possessed of a theme in the following manner. I am pushed by a natural need to set to work to write down the conversations that come into my head unaccountably. At first I hardly know the speakers, and cannot find names for them. Then they become more and more familiar, and I learn their names. Finally I come to know them very well, and discover what it is they are driving at, and why they have said and done the things I have been moved to set down.
>
> This is not being "guided by principles": it is hallucination; and sane hallucination is what we call play or drama.[11]

Long before writing *Saint Joan,* then, Shaw had a personal motive for wanting to learn how and why the imagination dramatizes its intuitions. A careful study of this passage reveals much about the extent to which his Vitalist theory is indebted to his dramatic practice. It is clear, for instance, that an impulse which comes to an individual "without reference to his own ends or interests" cannot plausibly be attributed to Darwinian natural selection, and Shaw's use of the word *inspiration* in this context suggests that "a creative effort of the imagination" can in fact come to us from sources which lie outside the range of Butlerian racial memory. Moreover, although the nature of those sources is not explained in the passage itself, the "natural need" to which it refers is clearly biological, and the fact that it is a "superpersonal" rather than a private need suggests that it must be a need of evolution. Thus the Life Force, like the God of Christianity, is able to enlighten the understanding of its agents without the aid of their physical senses.[12] "The garden is full of voices sometimes," Eve remarks in the first part of *Back to Methuselah*. "They put all sorts of thoughts into my head" (2: 4). By having Joan tell Baudricourt that it is through the imagination that the messages of God come to us, Shaw easily evaded the ontological confusions to which Joan's voices had condemned Twain.

Shaw's view that the voices were analogous to the creations of great imaginative writers is not especially original; it may be found, for example in Michelet.[13] But Shaw's Vitalism allowed him to go much farther than Michelet in defining the analogy between hallucination and poetry, for it allowed him to derive, from the Romantic doctrine of inspiration which they shared in common, an aesthetic which virtually identifies artistic creation with organic process.

The clearest exposition of Shaw's organic theory of art is Godfrey Kneller's verbal assault on Sir Isaac Newton in Shaw's drama *In Good King Charles's Golden Days* (written 1939). Kneller begins by denying that the normal path of a moving body is a straight line. After all, he reasons, although he is "the greatest draughtsman in Europe," even he cannot draw such a line without a ruler, and God does not own a ruler (6: 59-60). Moreover, even if He did He would not use it; for, as the straight line is a "dead thing," a cosmos made of it would be a mere piece of mechanical gadgetry instead of the clearly inspired piece of craftsmanship which every good artist perceives it to be:

> The line drawn by the artist's hand, the line that flows, that strikes, that speaks, that reveals! that is the line that shows the divine handiwork. [6: 63]

This suggests that among the characteristics which are shared in common by artistic and organic techniques of creation are freedom and spontaneity. In developing this idea Shaw appears to be relying on Bergson. Distinguishing between two kinds of order, Bergson at one point remarks, "The order of the second kind may be defined as geometry, which is its extreme limit; more generally, it is that kind of order that is concerned whenever a relation of necessary determination is found between causes and effects. It evokes ideas of inertia, of passivity, of automatism." But, he continues, the order of the first kind—that of vital phenomena—eschews both geometry and mechanism:

> Of a free action or a work of art we may say that they show a perfect order, and yet they can only be expressed in terms of ideas approximately, and after the event. Life in its entirety, regarded as creative evolution, is something analogous. [14]

Hence, Bergson concludes, scientific attempts to explain vital phenomena, to the extent that they rely upon mathematical abstraction, necessarily lead to distortion. [15] To this position Shaw adds that the artist, because his methods are the same as nature's, may normally be expected to anticipate the findings of the scientist. "Your Majesty: the world must learn from its artists because God made the world as an artist," Kneller at one point declares. "Your philosophers steal all their boasted discoveries from the artists; and then pretend they have deduced them from figures which they call equations, invented for that dishonest purpose." [16]

In short, Shaw held that inspiration is in general a more reliable source of new data than ratiocination, and that it normally precedes it. In answer to Dunois's remark that he would think that Joan were "a bit cracked" if she weren't able to give him sensible reasons for what she did, Joan replies, "Well, I have to find reasons for you, because you do not believe in my voices. But the voices come first; and I find the reasons after; whatever you may choose to believe" (2: 373). Yet, as Shaw recognized, the use of the method of inspiration is by no means a guarantee of success either in art or in science. Even if one accepts his view that "all truths, ancient or modern, are divinely inspired," one may still object, as he does, that "the instrument on which the inspiring force plays may be a very faulty one, and may even end, like Bunyan in The Holy War, by making the most ridiculous nonsense of his message." [17] Similarly, Shaw's use of the phrase "sane hallucination" to characterize drama is open to serious objection, for, as he frequently insists, most drama, like most visualizing, is merely escapist. [18] What was still needed then—and what Michelet in fact had failed to provide—was an objective criterion for distinguishing between hallucinations which are sane and those which are merely the result of mental infirmity. [19]

In furnishing such a criterion, Shaw may well have been influenced by Schopenhauer. He argues in *The World as Will and Representation* that "Imagination has been rightly recognized as an essential element of genius" since it "extends the mental horizon of the genius beyond the objects that actually present themselves to his person. . . ." But it does not follow, he adds, that "strength of imagination" is "evidence of genius." For just as a real object can be considered in two ways—either idealistically as it is in itself, or practically as it relates to other objects and to the will of the individual thinker—so also, can an imaginary one:

> Considered in the first way, it is a means to knowledge of the Idea, the communication of which is the work of art. In the second case, the imaginary object is used to build castles in the air, congenial to selfishness and to one's own whim, which for the moment delude and delight. . . . The man who indulges in this game is a dreamer; he will easily mingle with reality the pictures that delight his solitude, and will thus become unfit for real life. [20]

Similarly, Shaw advances three criteria to identify a hallucination as "sane." First, it will enable the mind to transcend the limitations imposed upon it by its dependence on perception; second, it will come to one "without reference to his own ends or interests"; [21] finally, being to that extent free from subjective distortion, it will not unfit one for constructive action in the real world. Thus, in 1914, in "Parents and Children," the preface to *Misalliance*, he distinguished two kinds of imagination: the "romantic," which he describes contemptuously as "the power to imagine things as they are not;" and the "realistic," which is "the power to imagine things as they are without actually sensing them." "The wise man," he explains, "knows that imagination is not only a means of pleasing himself and beguiling tedious hours with romances and fairy tales and fools' paradises . . . but also a means of foreseeing and being prepared for realities as yet unexperienced, and of testing the feasibility and desirability of serious Utopias" (4: 104-5).

Some years later Shaw presented the results of this inquiry into the imagination and its role in evolution in his "metabiological Pentateuch" *Bach to Methuselah* (written 1918 to 1920). He suggests that since "there is no such thing as the future until it is the present" (2: 199), the "realistic imagination" necessarily plays a vital role in all acts of creativity and invention. The hero—or rather heroine— of the first part of the work is the serpent, whom Shaw characteristically identifies with inspiration. [22] Being a mother herself she informs Eve of what one must do to give birth by asserting that "imagination is the beginning of creation." Before a thing can be created, she explains, it must first be desired; and since it does not yet exist, the imagination alone is capable of making it an object of desire. "You imagine what you desire: you will what you imagine; and at last you create what you will," she declares; and she points out in the same context that Eve originated in the mind of Lilith through "a marvelous story of something that never happened to a Lilith that never was."

The serpent then describes such stories as poems (2: 11), implying that nature's methods of creation are the same as those of poets. Hence the soundest insights into natural process are to be derived not from scientific textbooks but from "inspired human language." In the second part of the "Pentateuch," the enlightened Vitalist theologian Franklyn Barnabas asserts, "The poem is our real clue to biological science." "The most scientific document we possess at present," he explains, "is. . .the story of the Garden of Eden" (2: 74-78). By using that story to indicate that natural birth was "invented" by the Life Force in order to prepare life for "the pursuit of omnipotence and omniscience," Barnabas provides another valuable hint concerning the nature of the harmony which subsists between literary creation and organic process. As the method of the Life Force is the method of inspiration, so the fruits of the womb and those of the muse are alike in being expressions of the aspiration of life toward the unlimited perfection of God.[23]

This is the position Shaw had reached by 1920. Three years later he argued from it that "the figure Joan recognized as St Catherine was not really St Catherine, but the dramatization by Joan's imagination of that pressure upon her of the driving force that is behind evolution which I have just called the evolutionary appetite" (2: 276). His experience as a dramatist, reinforced by his Vitalist convictions, had carried him far beyond Galton to a highly original mystique of the role of the imagination in history.

THREE

JOAN AS VITALIST GENIUS

> *For the complete mysticism is that of the great Christian mystics. Let us leave aside, for the moment, their Christianity, and study in them the form apart from the matter. . .from their increased vitality there radiated an extraordinary energy, daring, power of conception and realization. . . . .Nearly all this superabundant activity was devoted to spreading the Christian faith. Yet there are exceptions, and the case of Joan of Arc will suffice to show that the form can be separated from the matter.*
>
> Bergson, *The Two Sources of Morality and Religion*

> *Though He slay me, yet will I trust in Him; but I will maintain my own ways before Him.*
> Job 13:15. Original epigraph to *Saint Joan*. Canceled by Shaw on the title page of his proof copy.

In 1936, after the filmscript of *Saint Joan* had been mutilated by a Catholic censor in Hollywood, Shaw wrote an angry letter to the *New York Times* in which he denied vehemently that there was anything anti-Catholic about his play. He maintained, it "was hailed by all instructed Catholics as a very unexpected first instalment of justice to the Church from Protestant quarters, and in effect, a vindication of the good faith of the famous trial at Rouen which had been held up to public execration for centuries as an abominable conspiracy. . . ."[1] It is a matter of historical fact, however, that Catholics have generally preferred to regard the Maid as a victim of such a conspiracy rather than as a martyr to Catholic anti-individualism. In 1934, when Shaw was actually at work on the ill-fated filmscript, one "instructed" Catholic, T. Laurason Riggs, complained in the *Commonweal* that those historians who have agreed with Shaw's opinion of Joan's trial have invariably assumed "that the Church must be the eternal enemy of any individual's claim to private inspiration, that she must attempt to crush it, and that the recognition of such inspiration is the peculiar prerogative of Protestantism and free thought."[2]

Shaw denied that this was his view. He declared in the same letter, echoing a remark he had made in the preface to *Saint Joan*, "The Church has a place for all types of character, including the ultra-Protestant. It admits that there are certain extraordinary persons to whom direct celestial revelations are vouchsafed" (2: 247). But as a defense of the Vatican against the reproach of anti-individualism this remark is rather disingenuous. Shaw had repeatedly insisted that what was at stake in Joan's dispute with her judges was nothing less than the doctrine of the infallibility of the pope and the historical Church in matters of faith and morals. Indeed, among the passages in the play to which the censor objected were two in which the Maid is chided by clerics for her intransigent defiances of ecclesiastical authority.[3]

Shaw's disagreement with the Vatican apparently results in part from a conviction that modern political and social problems are too complex to be dealt with adequately by those who are committed to an abstract moral code. But his most important objection seems to have been Vitalist. In "Parents and Children," after asserting that each child should be regarded as an experiment of the Life Force, he declares that the only way to ensure that such experiments not be spoiled through officious interference is to pass a law "that any person dictating a piece of conduct to a child or to anyone else as the will of God, or as absolutely right should be dealt with as a blasphemer: as, indeed, guilty of the unpardonable sin against the Holy Ghost." And he adds, "If the penalty were death, it would rid us at once of that scourge of humanity, the amateur Pope. As an Irish Protestant, I raise the cry of No Popery with hereditary zest. We are overrun with Popes" (4: 46).[4]

Thus, in spite of Shaw's protestations to the contrary, *Saint Joan* is a profoundly anti-Catholic play. Indeed, that fact is reflected in the very ideal of "saintly" behavior which it projects. But why, given his anti-Papist individualism, should Shaw have chosen to dramatize the career of a Catholic saint?

The answer apparently lies in his long-standing conviction that many of his Vitalist ideas had been arrived at intuitively by the great religious leaders of the past. As early as 1907, he concluded an account of those ideas by telling a Christian audience that they would find "a great deal of this truth" in the articles of the Church of England, in the Bible, and in "all of the religious books of the world."[5] The year after Joan was canonized he made the grounds of this conviction explicit in his 1921 preface to *Back to Methuselah*:

> Since the discovery of Evolution as the method of the Life Force, the religion of metaphysical Vitalism has been gaining the definiteness and concreteness needed to make it assimilable by the educated critical man. But it has always been with us. The popular religions, disgraced by their Opportunist cardinals and bishops, have been kept in credit by canonized saints whose secret was their conception of themselves as the instruments and vehicles of divine power and aspiration: a conception which at moments becomes an actual experience of ecstatic possession by that power. [2: lxxxiii-iv]

Hence, Shaw's choice in 1923 of a newly canonized saint for the subject of a heroic drama was, from his point of view, entirely appropriate. Indeed, he may even have seen that subject as an ideal opportunity to proselytize inasmuch as it enabled him to suggest that some, at least, of his own religious ideals and values were in agreement with those of Catholic Christendom.

For instance, he accepted the Catholic claim that, given her background, the Maid's spectacular success can be explained only on the supposition that she was a "saint," and therefore inspired. "If the historian is rationalist enough," he declares in the preface, "to deny that saints exist, and to hold that new ideas cannot come otherwise than by conscious ratiocination, he will never catch Joan's likeness" (2: 270). Because of this agreement with the Church, he was able to pay it the compliment of deriving his definition of *saint* from its criteria. "A saint," he observes, "is one who having practised heroic virtues, and enjoyed revelations or powers of the order which The Church classes technically as supernatural, is eligible for canonization"(2: 269-70).[6]

Shaw held, moreover, that what is fundamental to all religions is the belief in a higher power and the recognition of a responsibility to fulfill its purposes. Here he concurred with the Vatican in finding evidence of Joan's "heroic virtue" in the selflessness with which she devoted herself to the task which God had appointed for her. "But that there are forces at work," he declares, "which use individuals for purposes far transcending the purpose of keeping these individuals alive and prosperous and respectable and safe and happy . . . is established by the fact that men will, in the pursuit of knowledge and of social readjustments for which they will not be a penny the better, and are indeed often many pence the worse, face poverty, infamy, exile, imprisonment, dreadful hardship, and death" (2: 275-76).

But Shaw's conception of what it means to be a saint is still very far from being orthodox. Evidence of a disinterested and courageous commitment to "the pursuit of knowledge and of social readjustments" does not really constitute "heroic virtue" as that phrase is understood by the Vatican. The candidate for canonization (or, to use the Church's expression, the "servant of God") must also exhibit, in an exemplary manner, the three theological virtues of faith, hope, and charity.[7] Since Shaw rejected all three virtues as they are understood by Christians, he has taken no pains to endow his heroine with them. His remark in the preface, for example, that "her death was deliberately chosen as an alternative to life without liberty" (2: 283) suggests that it was an act of suicide rather than of martyrdom for the faith. In fact, the Catholic censor of the filmscript struck from that work everything which might convey the impression that her death was partly suicidal.[8]

Nor is this the only way in which Shaw's definition of the word *saint* is misleading. That the "revelations or powers" which confirm the sanctity of the servant of God be legitimately supernatural is not, for the Church, a merely technical requirement. It is an indispensable guarantee of the truth of the claim that he has received divine grace. For Catholic dogma holds not only that God cannot grant revelations or visions to mislead the faithful but also that unless such revelations come in fact from God they are not evidence of sanctity. So the same censor both cancelled Joan's remark to Baudricourt that it is through the imagination that the messages of God come from us, and struck from the text of the courtroom scene two lines in which she acknowledges that the failure of her voices since Compiegne may indicate that she has been "mocked by devils."[9]

Moreover, what is true of privileged revelations is true also of privileged powers. It is somewhat unorthodox to speak of the servant of God as "enjoying" either of them in the manner of a natural talent, for precisely what makes miracles of any sort valuable as evidence of sanctity is the presumption that only God can perform them.[10]

Built into the criteria for canonization, then, is the premise that, since the servant of God is an instrument of the divine will, his ultimate reliance must always have been upon God rather than upon himself. "The resolution of the righteous," Thomas à Kempis writes, "dependeth more upon the grace of God than upon their own wisdom; for in Him they always put their trust, whatsoever they take in hand. For man proposeth but God disposeth; and *the way of a man is not in himself*."[11] Such pious humility does not characterize Joan. In Dunois's words, she "thinks she has God in her pocket"—a phrase which also displeased the censor.[12] Indeed, so self-sufficient is she that at one point she refuses to appeal to God to accomplish what she thinks she can achieve herself by realistic, practical means. "I love church," she tells Dunois before the attack on Orleans, "but the English will not yield to prayers: they understand nothing but hard knocks and slashes. I will not go to church until we have beaten them" (2: 354).[13]

Underlying this pronouncement, which is certainly unorthodox coming from a saint, is Shaw's conviction that "man walking humbly before an external God is an ineffective creature compared to Man exploring as the instrument and embodiment of God with no other guide than the spark of divinity within him."[14] This view is clearly reflected in the ideal of saintliness presented in *Saint Joan*. Whereas temptation comes to the traditional Catholic saint as a prompting from the World, the Flesh, or the Devil to renounce the spiritual pilgrimage enjoined on him by God, it comes to Shaw's "Protestant" saint in the form of pressure from conventional morality to renounce the secular path which she has chosen for herself. She is tempted through her humility rather than through her pride.

Shaw also shows his disagreement with the Vatican in the preface, where he recasts his definition of *saint* in such a way as to make Joan's sainthood a function of her genius: "A genius is a person who, seeing farther and probing deeper than other people, has a different set of ethical valuations from theirs, and has energy enough to give effect to this extra vision and its valuations in whatever manner best suits his or her specific talents" (2: 269). He later explains that as such a union of moral originality and energy was bound to offend those whose duty it was to maintain the existing social order, Joan's genius ultimately brought her to the stake as a heretic (2: 292-93). The Church was able to make amends for burning her, however, through its recognition that "the highest wisdom may come as a divine revelation to an individual." Thus Shaw concludes that "as revelation may come by way of an enlightenment of the private judgment no less than by the words of a celestial personage appearing in a vision, a saint may be defined as a person of heroic virtue whose private judgment is privileged" (2: 294).

In short, Joan is a saint because she is a genius—or, in other words, an enlightened heretic. "Every genuine religious person," says *The*

Revolutionist's Handbook, "is a heretic and therefore a revolutionist" (4: 689). But moral originality is hardly a virtue to those who believe that the moral law is absolute and has been divinely revealed. In his preface Shaw virtually concedes that the Vatican would never have canonized Joan if it had agreed with him that her judges were justified in finding her guilty of heresy: "Her canonization was a magnificently Catholic gesture as the canonization of a Protestant saint by the Church of Rome. But its special value and virtue cannot be apparent *until it is known and understood as such*" (2: 299; my emphasis).

Shaw could not consistently claim to regard Joan as even an exemplary Christian, let alone a saint, for he had held throughout his career that no Christian can adopt the profession of arms without implicitly rejecting Christ. True, in the only passage in the play in which Joan indicates an awareness of the moral and doctrinal conflicts implied by her soldiership, he permits her to justify herself on a plea of patriotic nationalism. "We are all subject to the King of Heaven," she tells Baudricourt in the first scene, "and He gave us our countries and our languages, and meant us to keep them. If it were not so, it would be murder to kill an Englishman in battle; and you, squire, would be in great danger of hell fire" (2: 329). But if Shaw is right, no such plea can serve to vindicate Joan from the charge of hypocrisy. "When a bishop at the first shot," he declares in "Common Sense about the War," "abandons the worship of Christ, and rallies his flock around the altar of Mars, he may be acting patriotically, necessarily, manfully, rightly; but that does not justify him in pretending that there has been no change, and that Christ is, in effect, Mars."[15]

Even in her nationalism, according to Shaw, Joan was a heretic. In that matter also she carried her reliance on her private judgment to the point of defying the authority of the Church. "She objected to foreigners," he declares in the preface, "on the sensible ground that they were not in their proper place in France; but she had no notion of how this brought her into conflict with Catholicism and Feudalism, both essentially international" (2: 285). In the course of the famous interview in scene four Shaw makes Cauchon tell Warwick, "To her the French-speaking people are what the Holy Scriptures describe as a nation. Call this side of her heresy Nationalism if you will: I can find you no better name for it. I can only tell you that it is essentially anti-Catholic and anti-Christian; for the Catholic Church knows only one realm, and that is the realm of Christ's kingdom. Divide that kingdom into nations, and you dethrone Christ" (2: 369).

Yet it is precisely in her nationalism that Joan gives the most convincing evidence of her "genius". Here Shaw succeeds not only in emphasizing the soundness of her opinions but also in defining their moral originality. This he accomplishes largely by contrasting them with those of the English chaplain, John de Stogumber, a jingoist simpleton who complains of her that she "denies to England her legitimate conquests, given her by God because of her peculiar fitness to rule over less civilized races for their own good" (2: 369-70). "Seeing farther and probing deeper" than that zealous cleric, Joan reveals her "genius" in her inspired recognition of two truths which Shaw, as an Irishman, claimed to have learned from experience: that every nation has a natural right to self-government, and that no army of occupation, no matter how necessary a given set of historical circumstances may appear to make it, can, in itself, be otherwise than pernicious. "If I went into England," she tells Baudricourt, "against the will of God to conquer England, and tried to live there and speak its language, the devil would enter into me; and when I was old I should shudder to remember the wickednesses I did" (2: 330-31).

This enlightened nationalism rests, in turn, on an ideal which Shaw apparently regards as a still more convincing proof of Joan's genius: an inspired conception of the state as an instrument of the will of God.[16] And it is to this last idea, Shaw suggests, rather than to her Catholic piety, that Joan owed the bulk of that "energy" which enabled her to "give effect to [her] extra vision and its valuations." By 1903 Shaw had pointed out in *Man and Superman* that men are cowards when they are motivated only by self-interest. As his Don Juan puts it, they "never really overcome fear until they imagine they are fighting to further a universal purpose—fighting for an idea, as they call it" (3: 622).[17] Joan's "idea," as the English commander Warwick describes it, is the essentially "Protestant" conception "that the kings should give their realms to God, and then reign as God's bailiffs" (2: 367). Joan's success in impressing others with the attractiveness of this "Protestant" idea enables her not only to put new heart into the demoralized army of France (2: 331) but also to inspire France's inveterately timid monarch with the courage he needs to back her at the risk of antagonizing his counsellors (2: 348).

What makes this idea of the Maid's a "Protestant" one for Shaw is that it is anti-feudal—the point being, as Warwick explains it, that Joan's resistance to the authority of the feudal aristocracy is of a piece with her resistance to the authority of the Church. "These two ideas of hers," he tells Cauchon, "are the same idea at bottom. It goes deep, my Lord. It is the protest of the individual soul against the interference of priest or peer between the private man and his God" (2: 368-69). This observation suggests still another respect in which Shaw's notion of religious vocation differs from that of Catholicism. Traditionally, Catholic ideals of such vocation have tended to frown on political radicalism. Convinced as he was that the end of the world was at hand, Jesus advised his followers to concern themselves with their own salvation rather than with the reform of society, with the result that the emphasis in his teaching is almost entirely psychological rather than political. But Joan, by contrast, is much more exclusively concerned with the state of the realm than with that of her soul. Shaw attempted to meet this objection by arguing that whenever the state comes between "the private man and his God" his personal salvation must depend upon revolutionary political action. But this argument also failed to satisfy his Catholic censor. That official, coming to Joan's injunction to Baudricourt that "you must not think about your duty to your feudal lord, but about your duty to God," emended it to read, "but more about your duty to God."[18]

In spite of the title, then, Shaw has taken no pains in his play to represent Joan as being, in any orthodox sense, a saint. On the contrary, his characterization of her has been guided throughout by the heretical view he expressed in the preface to *Back to Methuselah*: that man must be his own providence and that, consequently, his salvation lies in his own political keeping. "If Man is to be saved," he declares, "Man must save himself" (2: xvii).

FOUR

JOAN AS PROTESTANT

*It would indeed be easy for these crafty and dangerous
sowers of deceitful inventions to infect the Catholic people, if everyone, without the approbation and consent of
our Holy Mother Church, were free to invent supernatural revelations at his own pleasure, and could usurp
the authority of God and His saints . . . . Wherefore it
was clearly recognized by all how dangerous it was, how
fearful, to give too light credence to the modern inventions
which have for some time past been scattered in this most
Christian Kingdom, not by this woman only, but by many
others also; and all the faithful of the Christian religion
must be warned by such a sad example not to act so hastily
after their own desires, but to listen to the teachings of the
Church and the instruction of the prelates rather than the
fables of superstitious women. For if we are at last
through our own faults arrived at the point where witches
falsely prophesying in God's name but without His authority, are better received by the frivolous people than
pastors and doctors of the Church to whom Christ for-
merly said, "Go ye and teach the nations," the end is
come, religion will perish, faith is in decay, the Church is
trampled underfoot and the iniquity of Satan dominates
the whole world.*

The Trial of Jeanne d'Arc

*Nothing seems more immoral than the morality of the
future. We are not judges of what is to come.*
France, "*La Morale et la Science: M. Paul Bourget,*" no. 3.

The Archbishop remarks to La Tremouille, in what is undoubtedly
the most celebrated dialogue in *Saint Joan*, that a miracle is an event
which creates faith. "That is the purpose and nature of miracles. They
may seem very wonderful to the people who witness them, and very
simple to those who perform them. That does not matter, if they
confirm or create faith they are true miracles." When La Tremouille
protests that at that rate there is no distinction between a miracle and a
fraud, the Archbishop replies, in effect, that all government depends

upon just such a fraud: "Well, the Church has to rule men for the good of their souls as you have to rule them for the good of their bodies. To do that, the Church must do as you do: nourish their faith by poetry" (2: 340-41).

The key to the significance of this interchange is provided in *The Perfect Wagnerite*, where Shaw attacks the Hobbesian idea that men's passions would make them wholly ungovernable were it not that their reason renders them amenable to legal control. The truth is that men, so far from being governable through their reason, will not submit to any authority whatever that does not proceed by "deliberately filling them with prejudices and practising on their imaginations."[1] He implies that the power of the historical Church has always depended upon its recognition of this fact. But the trouble with governing by such means is that once respect for a given law has been inculcated as a superstition, it becomes impossible to alter that law without provoking the fanatic opposition of the masses—with the result that the lawmakers themselves become slaves of the very makeshifts they have created to secure their power (*Works* 19: 186-87).[2] It is from this fact, he concludes, that the need for "Protestantism" arises—the need, that is, for men with sufficient moral and intellectual courage to "protest" against attempts to impose upon them any authority apart from the will of God (*Works* 19: 225-26).

Thus Shaw accepted early in his career the Romantic doctrine that humanity can save itself only by repudiating ethical training or "conscience" in favor of its own benevolent impulses. "The world has always delighted in the man who is delivered from conscience," he remarks in *The Perfect Wagnerite* (*Works* 19: 225). And later in the same chapter, "Siegfried as Protestant," he adds, "The most inevitable dramatic conception, then, of the nineteenth century is that of a perfectly naive hero upsetting religion, law and order in all directions, and establishing in their place the unfettered action of Humanity doing exactly what it likes, and producing order instead of confusion thereby because it likes to do what is necessary for the good of the race" (*Works* 19: 228).

"Protestantism," then, has emerged historically as a "protest" against wrong-headed attempts to maintain authority by irrationalist methods. But it does not follow, Shaw maintains, that it is itself rationalistic. One correspondent attempted to refute Shaw's claim that Joan was the first Protestant by pointing out that as early as the ninth century Johannes Scotus Erigena had opposed his reason to the dogmatism of the Vatican. Shaw replied that Erigenist rationalism was not historic Protestantism, and that Joan's maxim, "God must be served first," by which she sought to assert the superiority of her private judgment to the authority of the Church, was completely irrational.[3]

Clearly this remark implies that irrationalism is not only an inseparable feature of the Protestant mentality but is also closely related to what Shaw regards as Protestant anti-authoritarianism. But the example of Erigena indicates just as clearly that one may rebel against authority without denying the sovereignty of reason; it is not by virtue of his anti-authoritarianism that the Protestant is an irrationalist. On the contrary, it is precisely his irrationalism that makes him anti-authoritarian. As the phrase "God must be served first" suggests, his reliance upon direct inspiration is bound to put him at odds with the "religion, law and order" of his time.

Hence, from the very beginning Shaw conceived of his play as one which would show "the Church, the Inquisition, the Feudal System, with divine inspiration always beating against their too inelastic limits" (2: 312). And behind his interest in the subject, accordingly, lay his conviction that if the anti-mystical rationalism which was dominating Western civilization in his time were not to end by destroying that civilization altogether, it must be rescued by a prophet who was himself sufficiently inspired to succeed in returning his fellows to a sense of religious purpose. "We want a few mad people now," Shaw makes Poulengy remark in the first scene of *Saint Joan*. "See where the sane ones have landed us!" (2: 327).[4] When his friends the Hamons flubbed their French translation of that line, he warned them that it had been taken by readers and audiences as an allusion to the war of 1914-1918, and therefore had to close with more crispness than their "ceux qui sont sains d'esprit."[5]

Shaw, in choosing a "Protestant" as the subject for a heroic drama, then, was responding to what he took to be the urgent needs of the modern world. Yet in the very process of making this point he sometimes implies that the sort of rationalism with which Joan was forced to contend in the fifteenth century was very different form the atheistic materialism which her like would have to confront in the twentieth. In the preface he concluded a long attack against modern rationalism by declaring, "To Joan and her contemporaries we should appear as a drove of Gadarene swine, possessed by all the unclean spirits cast out by the faith and civilization of the Middle Ages, running violently down a steep place into a hell of high explosives" (2: 279).

From this it appears that modern rationalism differs from medieval in being fundamentally godless; and in fact, it is clear from a number of Shaw's remarks on the subject that he did not believe that rationalism need be materialistic.[6] In the 1915 preface to *Androcles and the Lion*, for example, he describes St. Paul as "an inveterate Roman Rationalist, always discarding the irrational real thing for the unreal but ratiocinable postulate" (5: 396). And that account of Paul's views suggests that a rationalist in theology is one who, instead of turning directly to God for guidance, attempts to arrive at both his ethics and his metaphysics by theorizing about the implications of a given body of traditional doctrine.

So conceived, however, theological rationalism does share one important feature in common with materialism: it represents an attempt to substitute the counsel of dogmatic "reason" for that of inspiration in the conduct of the moral life. To that extent it is very nearly as wrong-headed as materialism itself is, being rooted in an idealistic misconception of the reason which regards that faculty as transcendent and absolute and thus comes ultimately to identify it with God.

The problem with this view, according to Shaw, is that it simply is not consistent with what we now know about the biological origin of reason. Modern science has taught us that reason, so far from being eternal and transcendent, is a relatively recent product of evolution which has been developed in certain organisms by the Life Force to serve purposes that are entirely practical. Thus, its exercise from the beginning has always been subordinate to and dependent on that of the will; for that reason, Shaw argues, it follows that there is actually no distinction between reasoning and rationalizing. "We are only just discovering," he wrote in 1944, "that there is such a thing as wishful thinking; but the Creative Evolutionist knows that all thinking is wishful, and that we cannot think until our wishes or fears or cupidities or curiosities create what we call attention."[7]

This being the case, the substitution of reason for inspiration in the conduct of the moral life inevitably means the substitution of the personal will of the governors for the "superpersonal" will of God. "Law is blind without counsel," Shaw has Jesus declare in the Jesus-Pilate Scene, "The counsel men agree with is vain: it is only the echo of their own voices. A million echoes will not help you to rule righteously."[8]

Hence, as Shaw is careful to indicate in his play, Joan has no choice but to seek counsel directly and exclusively from God, which in practice means that she must rely for guidance entirely upon her own inspiration. The inevitable result is that even her friends come to regard her as unreasonably and incorrigibly self-willed. When they finally indicate this by turning against her ("all the voices that come to you," declares the Archbishop in the cathedral scene, "are the echoes of your own wilfulness"), she responds by declaring bitterly, "There is no help, no counsel, in any of you":

> I see now that the loneliness of God is His strength: what would He be if He listened to your jealous little counsels? Well, my loneliness shall be my strength, too: it is better to be alone with God: His friendship will not fail me, nor His counsel, nor His love. [2: 380-82]

For Shaw's Joan, then, as for his Jesus, "the greatest of God's names is Counsellor. . . ."[9]

One corollary to this irrationalist position is that mere reasonableness must count for nothing in the search for truth, since a skillful debater can argue with equal cogency on both sides of any question. "You cannot impose on me with your reasonable and well-informed opinion," Jesus tells Pilate. "If it is your will to crucify me, I can find you a dozen reasons for doing so; and your police can supply you with a hundred facts to support the reasons. If it is your will to spare me I can find you just as many reasons for that; and my disciples will supply you with more facts than you have time or patience to listen to. That is why your lawyers can plead as well for one side as another, and can therefore plead without dishonor for the side that pays them, like the hackney charioteer who will drive you north as readily as south for the same fare" (5: 516-17).

Nowhere in Shaw's work is this attitude dramatized more effectively than in the famous defense of "religion, law and order" made by the Inquisitor in the trial scene of *Saint Joan*.[10] With its tirade against those "vain and ignorant persons" who set up "their own judgment against The Church," the speech is intended to be a vindication of the "essential mercy" of the Inquisition in preserving society from the anarchy which would result if radicals like Joan were countenanced (2: 391-94). As such, it is conducted with great brilliance and rhetorical skill. But as Joan remarks, "There is. . .sometimes great foolishness in the wisdom of scholars" (2: 402-3),[11] and all of the Inquisitor's plausibility serves merely to confirm Shaw's anti-rationalist claim that "there are just as good reasons for burning a heretic at the stake as for rescuing a ship-wrecked crew from drowning—in fact, there are better."[12]

This is not to say, however, that the Inquisitor's reasoning is, as reasoning, unsound. He is correct in pointing out that there are false prophets as well as true, that like the true they also claim to be divinely inspired, and that they are on that account a serious threat to the commonwealth. But the soundness of his reasoning cannot rescue him from the falsity of his position, which requires him to distinguish between the two without being divinely inspired himself. To be sure, the Inquisitor has the support of Joan's party in complaining that she will not listen to "reason." But Shaw's point is that she cannot do so without a cowardly betrayal of her intuitions, since it is of the essence of genius to transcend mere rationality. Shaw says in *The Revolutionist's Handbook*, "The man who listens to Reason is lost: Reason enslaves all whose minds are not strong enough to master her" (3: 739). Hence the tragicomic irony that informs the whole scene: the very limitations in the reason which make the vocation of such prophets as Joan necessary also render the problem faced by merely "reasonable" people like the Inquisitor virtually insoluble.

Traditionally, of course, the Church had attempted to solve that problem by referring it to the personal conduct of any given prophet, reasoning that no one could really be inspired by the Holy Ghost who was not himself exemplary in that respect. But to assume this, Shaw believed, is to fall victim to a fallacy comparable to that of the rationalist: that the dictates of morality are transcendent and absolute and are therefore the same at all times. Shaw held, consistently with his Vitalism, that the so-called moral laws are similar to those of logic in being products of man's evolution which he must transcend if he is to surpass his present level of development. This, indeed, is the moral to be drawn from the Inquisitor's wrong-headed insistence on Joan's masculine dress. Inspiration, by the same token that it is irrational, must also be immoral: in matters of conscience as in those of the intellect, it cannot permit itself to be confined.[13]

Mere morality, then, like mere reasonableness, proves to be of no use to men like the Inquisitor in distinguishing the true prophet from the false. Yet the distinction must be made for all that; if, on the one hand, "it is necessary for the welfare of society that genius should be privileged to utter sedition, to blaspheme, to outrage good taste," on the other hand, "it is idle to demand unlimited toleration of apparently outrageous conduct on the plea that the offender is a genius."[14]
The result is that the leaders of society are confronted with what appears to be an unresolvable dilemma. "The more closely we grapple with it," Shaw declares in his preface, "the more difficult it becomes"

(2: 301). And it is a fact that he had been grappling with it without success for more than thirty years.

Thus as early as 1891 Shaw had pointed out in *The Quintessence of Ibsenism* that the inspired pioneer in morals must expect to encounter more hostility from the conscientious people in his community than from the mass of its unregenerate "Philistines."[15] As late as 1924, with *Saint Joan* and its preface behind him, he advised "The Intelligent Woman" in her *Guide to Socialism and Capitalism* that she cannot breed for good children because she does not know what a good child is:

> Energetic, imaginative, enterprising, brave children are never out of mischief from their parents' point of view. And grown-up geniuses are seldom liked until they are dead. Considering that we poisoned Socrates, crucified Christ, and burnt Joan of Arc amid popular applause, because, after a trial by responsible lawyers and Churchmen, we decided that they were too wicked to be allowed to live, we can hardly set up to be judges of goodness or to have any sincere liking for it.[16]

Apparently, then, Shaw's study of Joan's career had tended to make him skeptical about the ability of inspired religious teachers to induce his fellows to undertake necessary political and social reforms.[17] But if Joan's protestantizing efforts had failed, in Shaw's opinion, to produce that respect for the private inspiration of saints and prophets which the word *Protestant* implied, the fact of that failure might nevertheless be used to drive home some important historical lessons.

In reading those lessons to a Church which Shaw describes in the preface as "not yet Catholic enough" (2: 298), he insists that no organization in which advancement depends upon the selection of a superior by his inferiors can "compete successfully in the selection of its principals with the direct choice of the Holy Ghost as it flashes with unerring aim upon the individual." Hence, he argues, the saints and prophets "are always really self-selected, like Joan"; and if the Vatican is to avoid the disastrous mistake of persecuting them, it must "make it a point of honor to privilege heresy to the last bearable degree on the simple ground that all evolution in thought and conduct must at first appear as heresy and misconduct" (2: 300).

The Church in other words must either abandon its moral absolutism in favor of an evolutionary ethic which will recognize the need for "Protestantism" in the ethical progress of the race or run the risk of forfeiting its own effectiveness as a spiritual force by suppressing its natural leaders. But the Maid, as Shaw was aware, was as much an absolutist as her judges, and was certainly no less intolerant (5: 510).[18] "St. Joan did not claim toleration," he remarks in the 1933 preface to *On the Rocks*: "she was so far from believing in it that she wanted to lead a crusade of extermination against the Husites, though she was burnt for sharing their heresy. That is how all the martyrs have missed the point of their defence. They all claimed to possess absolute truth as against the error of their persecutors, and would have considered it their duty to persecute for its sake if they had had the power" (5: 510). Moreover, Shaw himself was unable to provide an objective criterion for determining the proper limits of toleration. Since, as Joan's fate indicates, "we can hardly set up to be judges of goodness," the problems involved in identifying prophets like her and providing them with appropriate influence remain as intractable as ever:

> O God that madest this beautiful earth, when will it be ready to receive Thy saints? How long, O Lord, how long?

FIVE

JOAN AS MARTYR TO THE LIFE FORCE

*They have called "God" what was contrary to them and
gave them pain. . . . And they did not know how to love
their god except by crucifying man.*
Nietzsche, *Thus Spoke Zarathustra*

Shaw felt a lifelong antipathy toward Christian self-denial and
self-sacrifice. In 1891 he attacked the ideal of duty, in the first chapter
of *The Quintessence of Ibsenism*, arguing that it is essentially conservative. A man can escape from its "tyranny," he asserted, only when he
has repudiated his duty to God and to society, so that "a sense at last
arises in him of his duty to himself." He arrived at this position in
reaction against Christian asceticism. Of all forms of duty worship, he
held, the most destructive is that which, originating in the fear of God,
turns men into moral monsters through the persistent starvation of
their senses and emotions:

> Duty arises at first, a gloomy tyranny, out of man's helplessness,
> his self-mistrust, in a word, his abstract fear. He personifies all
> that he abstractly fears as God, and straightway becomes the slave
> of his duty to God. He imposes that slavery fiercely on his chil-
> dren, threatening them with hell, and punishing them for their
> attempts to be happy.[1]

Given these views, Shaw necessarily had no patience with the
doctrine of the atonement. In fact, his antipathy to the crucifixion
seems to have resulted largely from the contempt he felt for the notion
of heroism for which it stands. His view, as it is expressed in the note
to *Caesar and Cleopatra*, was that "the way to produce an impression of
greatness is by exhibiting a man, not as mortifying his nature by
doing his duty. . .but as simply doing what he naturally wants to
do."[2] Yet one may easily object to this ideal of "heroic virtue" that, by
contrast with the Christian ideal, it must tend to encourage an un-
generous solicitude for the preservation of one's own life. "Greater
love hath no man than this," said Jesus to his disciples during the Last

Supper, "that a man lay down his life for his friends." But can the man who does so reasonably be said to be doing "what he naturally wants to do"?

In the thirty-three years between the writing of *The Quintessence of Ibsenism* and that of *Saint Joan*, Shaw made a number of attempts to explore this question in plays which throw a good deal of light upon his handling of the Maid's commitment. The first attempt appeared in the very play which most effectively dramatizes the excesses of a mistaken sense of religious duty. In *The Devil's Disciple* (1897) Shaw's protagonist, Richard Dudgeon, acquires his reputation as a Satanist largely because of his antipathy to the Christian ideal of self-sacrifice. Yet he allows himself to be sentenced to death for the crime of another. In explaining his motives to the wife of the man he saved, he points out that a man's willingness to give his life for a generous purpose may be the result not of self-effacement but of an irresistible inner impulse of self-respect. "What I did last night," he tells her, "I did in cold blood, caring not half so much for your husband, or. . .for you . . . as I do for myself. I had no motive and no interest: all I can tell you is that when it came to the point whether I would take my neck out of the noose and put another man's into it, I could not do it. . . .I have been brought up standing by the law of my own nature; and I may not go against it, gallows or no gallows" (3: 322).

Shaw claimed in *The Quintessence of Ibsenism* that when "the tyranny of duty" has been broken, "the man's God is himself; and he, self-satisfied at last, ceases to be selfish."[3] Dudgeon, having repudiated his duty to God in order to follow "the law of his own nature," becomes more generous than his Puritan mother, who, in the process of sacrificing everything to the Lord, has hardened her heart against her fellowman. Ironically, he also becomes more devout. For what most distinguishes the truly religious man from such sanctimonious bigots as Mrs. Dudgeon is the knowledge that love for God is not in fact inconsistent with love for oneself, and that the genuine religious spirit actually regards the service of the Lord as a source of fulfillment. "That is the essence of religion," Shaw later remarked, "to be working for things outside yourself, and it is not sacrifice. You are living far more abundantly because of it."[4]

Shaw had no difficulty, then, in reconciling his repudiation of the Christian ideal of sacrifice with his conviction that the truly religious life is one of disinterested service. But he could not plausibly claim that Dick's heroic acceptance of death had been intended merely as a means of attaining fulfillment. How, after all, could a man to whom

religion had brought a more abundant life "naturally want" to renounce it? Hence in defending the work three years later in the
preface to *Three Plays for Puritans* he was unable to answer the objection of his critics that Dick's heroism was not plausibly motivated (3:
li). It will not suffice merely to point out that in real life such actions are
often inexplicable even to their performers. That fact itself needs to be
psychologically explained. If Dick is acting under compulsion, what is
the nature of that compulsion? How, if not from the approval of his
fellows, does the disciple of the devil acquire his self-respect? And
what, if not the desire for happiness or the instinct for self-
preservation, is the "law" of such a man's nature?

Shortly after the turn of the century Shaw was arguing the failure of
rationalism to answer such questions in favor of his anti-Benthamite
view that men are instruments of a purpose which is independent of
and indifferent to their merely personal desires. In 1907 he told a
Christian audience at the Kensington Town Hall that materialism
cannot account for the evidence of design in nature. "The religious
people naturally turn this argument to account, saying, 'it is all very
well to say that life is a mere pursuit of pleasure and gain, but many
men do not live in order to get a balance of pleasure over pain; you see
everywhere men doing work that does not benefit them—they call it
God's work; natural selection cannot account for that. There is behind
the universe an intelligent and driving force of which we ourselves are
a part—a divine spark.'"[5]

Two years after the Kensington Hall lecture, in dramatizing the
"shewing-up" of his Western badman, Blanco Posnet, Shaw reworked the theme of *The Devil's Disciple* in the light of this Vitalist
conviction. Like Dick, Blanco thinks of himself with pride as an
enemy of God, for he too has been revolted by the flagrant hypocrisy
of his so-called Christian neighbors. And like Dick, who becomes a
Satanist largely in reaction against his Puritan mother, he directs the
brunt of his Mephistophelian scorn toward a member of his immediate family. For Blanco's brother, an imperfectly reformed rascal
who calls himself "The Elder Daniels," is endowed with just that
combination of greed and sanctimoniousness that had characterized
Mrs. Dudgeon. Indeed, in one way Daniels's hypocrisy is even more
insidious than hers, because in his case the idea of resistance to
temptation is made a cloak not merely for selfishness but also for an
inveterate fear of life. Thus he justifies his lucrative trade in spirits on
the grounds that "what keeps America to-day the purest of the nations

is that when she's not working she's too drunk to hear the voice of the tempter" (5: 253). But for Shaw—who held that "temptation and inspiration mean the same thing"—this attitude toward "the tempter" is tantamount to a craven denial of the Holy Ghost.[6] So he takes pains in his play to make the "shewing-up" of his protagonist an illustration of the point that a man may be "tempted" for his own good. Shortly before stealing a horse from Daniels, Blanco meets a woman who desperately needs to get her ailing child to a doctor. He knows that without the horse he cannot avoid being caught and hanged for his theft. But when the life in the child calls out to the life in him, he discovers that "there are forces at work which use individuals for purposes far transcending the purpose of keeping these individuals alive and prosperous. . . and safe and happy. . . ." (2: 275-76). "He made me," he moralizes later, "because He had a job for me. He let me run loose till the job was ready; and then I had to come along and do it, hanging or no hanging" (5: 274).

When Shaw, in 1912, turned for the first time to the subject of Christian martyrdom, he resumed the position he had worked out in those two earlier plays. The heroine of *Androcles and the Lion*, Lavinia, admits that it is not easy for her and her fellow Christians to die, since "our faith makes life far stronger and more wonderful in us than when we walked in darkness and had nothing to live for" (5: 437). But she accepts her fate nevertheless, and for motives which are very much like those of Dick and Blanco. They are similarly compulsive and similarly self-respecting. And since the doctrine of the afterlife appears to be one of the Christian "stories and dreams" which she repudiates as death approaches, they are even similarly disinterested (5: 462-63).[7] What is more, in explaining those motives to the handsome Roman captain, who attempts to persuade her to save herself by dropping a pinch of incense on the altar of Diana, she reveals that she is as contemptuous as Dick and Blanco had been of the bigotry and hyprocrisy which result from a wrongheaded sense of religious duty:

> Oh, do you think that I, a woman, would quarrel with you for
> sacrificing to a woman god like Diana, if Diana meant to you what
> Christ means to me? No: we should kneel side by side before her
> altar like two children. But when men who believe neither in my
> god nor in their own—men who do not know the meaning of the
> word religion—when these men drag me to the foot of an iron
> statute that has become the symbol of the terror and darkness
> through which they walk, of their cruelty and greed, of their
> hatred of God and their oppression of man—when they ask me to

pledge my soul before the people that this hideous idol is God,
and that all this wickedness and falsehood is divine truth, I cannot
do it, not if they could put a thousand cruel deaths on me. I tell
you, it is physically impossible. [5: 439-40]

What makes it impossible, of course, is that, Lavinia, like Blanco, is in
the grip of a power that transcends her own rational desires. "Well,
Captain," she explains, "if I took a pinch of incense in my hand and
stretched it out over the altar fire, my hand would come back. My body
would be true to my faith even if you could corrupt my mind" (5: 440).

Superficially Joan's behavior in the face of death appears quite
unlike that of these three fictive characters. When she was offered the
opportunity to save herself by backing down she, unlike Dick and
Lavinia, did not refuse on the grounds that "the law of her nature"
made her compliance physically impossible. On the contrary, "when
it became evident that she had miscalculated: when she was led to the
stake, and La Hire was not thundering at the gates of Rouen nor
charging Warwick's men at arms, she threw over Saint Catherine at
once, and recanted." Nor, in Shaw's opinion, was her subsequent
"relapse" particularly disinterested: "It was not until she discovered
that she had gained nothing by her recantation but close imprisonment for life that she withdrew it, and deliberately and explicitly
chose burning instead: a decision which shewed not only the extraordinary decision of her character, but also a Rationalism carried to its
ultimate human test of suicide" (2: 280).

Nevertheless, the ideal of heroic commitment which Shaw worked
out in these three early plays clearly exerted a great deal of influence on
his version of his heroine's martyrdom. Indeed, even his handling of
her recantation seems to have been affected by it, for she did not
perform that action without a sharp internal struggle. In a significant
stage direction he observes that in the act of signing, Joan was
"tormented by the rebellion of her soul against her mind and body" (2: 406);
that remark, when translated into the vocabulary of Shavian Vitalism,
apparently means that her denial of her evolutionary mission was
tantamount to a denial of life. For Shaw accepted from Samuel Butler
the idea that the soul is "an etherial, spiritual, vital principle, apart
from matter, which, nevertheless, it animates,"[8] and he applied this
definition in such a way as to suggest that the potentiality for commitment to the needs of evolution is one of the conditions of life itself.
He explairs in a program note to *Don Juan in Hell* that what "modern
theology" understands by *the soul* is "not an organ like the liver, but
the divine element common to all life, which causes us 'to do the will

of God' in addition to looking after our individual interests, and to honor one another solely for our divine activities and not at all for our selfish activities" (3: 744).

Presumably, then, Joan's motive for accepting death was the same as Dick's and Blanco's and Lavinia's. The pressure of the Life Force upon her was such that she literally could not help herself. But here it may be objected that the fact that she recanted at all is conclusive evidence that she was acting under no such compulsion. This objection suggests another which, from a Vitalist point of view at least, is still more fundamental; How can we account, in terms of Shavian biology, for the conflict between Joan's flesh and the vital spirit that animates it? If the recoiling of Lavinia's hand from the altar of Diana indicates that the non-rational impulses of the body are enlisted on behalf of the soul, how does it happen that Joan's soul finds itself in "rebellion" against her body?

The answer to this question lies apparently in the dualism of life and matter which is implied both by Butler's definition of the soul as a "vital principle" and Shaw's description of it as "the divine element common to all life." At the conclusion of *Back to Methuselah* Lilith, whom Shaw identifies with the Life Force, declares, "I brought life into the whirlpool of force, and compelled my enemy, Matter, to obey a living soul. But in enslaving Life's enemy I made him Life's master; for that is the end of all slavery. . ." (2: 262). In terms of this doctrine, the recoiling of Lavinia's hand from the altar of Diana apparently indicates that Matter, in a living organism, is the slave of Life, while the rebellion of Joan's soul against her body reveals that even when thus enslaved Matter is still Life's enemy. As long as Lilith is compelled to depend upon Matter for the fulfillment of her aims, her children will necessarily by endowed with personal desires, such as the desire to survive as individual organisms, which must sometimes conflict with her own "superpersonal" aspirations.

At all events, Shaw's handling in the play proper of the episode in which Joan recants her recantation clearly suggests that he conceived of that act as a stirring reaffirmation of the life she has just denied. He contrives to make her motive for "relapsing" a test of the strength of another conviction which she shares with Dick and Lavinia: since the truly religious spirit is one that seeks the utmost possible fulfillment in life, any attempt to deny such fulfillment either to oneself or to another is inherently atheistic:

> You promised me my life; but you lied. You think that life is

nothing but not being stone dead. . . . I could do without my war
horse; I could drag about in a skirt; I could let the banners and the
trumpets and the knights and soldiers pass me and leave me
behind as they leave the other women, if only I could still hear the
wind in the trees, the larks in the sunshine. . .and the blessed
blessed church bells that send my angel voices floating to me on
the wind. But without these things I cannot live: and by your
wanting to take them away from me, or from any human creature,
I know that your counsel is of the devil, and that mine is of
God.[9] [2:407]

The Church, Shaw suggests in his preface, might have allowed Joan to
go free if it had not been "deeply corrupted, as all the Churches were
and still are, by primitive Calibanism (in Browning's sense), or the
propitiation of a dreaded deity by suffering and sacrifice" (2: 297).

Finally, Shaw implies that long before Joan's capture, she, like Dick
and Blanco and Lavinia, must have foreseen her martyrdom, and that
she accepted it, as they did, in obedience to the law of her nature.
Thus, in the fifth scene of the play, at the point where the leaders of her
party turn against her at last, he makes her declare,

I see now that the loneliness of God is His strength: what would
He be if He listened to your jealous little counsels? Well, my
loneliness shall be my strength too: it is better to be alone with
God: His friendship will not fail me, nor His counsel, nor His
love. In His strength I will dare, and dare, and dare, until I die. I
will go out now to the common people, and let the love in their
eyes comfort me for the hate in yours. You will all be glad to see me
burnt; but if I go through the fire I shall go through it to their
hearts for ever and ever. And so, God be with me! [2: 382]

This speech, which reflects Shaw's ever-deepening conviction that
"good-natured unambitious men are cowards when they have no
religion,"[10] is clearly the most moving expression in the whole play of
the devotional impulse underlying the Maid's commitment. Yet for all
its religious fervor, it is subtly unorthodox. In it, Joan not only pre-
sumes on the continued favor of God, but she even proposes to
emulate his self-sufficiency. This presumption, together with the fact
that she shows more solicitude here for the fate of her reputation in
this world than for that of her soul in the next, suggests that in Shaw's
opinion her "heroic virtue" proceeded not so much from Christian
faith as from personal pride.

Thus, even where Shaw insists upon the distinctively religious
character of the Maid's aspirations, he is careful not to give the

impression that she was acting in conformity with the Christian ideal of sacrifice. Indeed, he implies that she, unlike Jesus, did not claim to be laying down her life for her friends, and that she went to the stake largely in response to the irresistible demands of her own self-esteem.

SIX

THE TRUE JOY IN LIFE

*It was also just that he should have given them a God in
exchange for those which he had taken from them, for
those who destroy hope in men are cruel.*
France, *Pierre Nozière*

Of the three books concerning Joan of Arc which we have examined
in this text, *Saint Joan* is clearly the most satisfying. Shaw, in keeping
with his view that "the best dramatic art is the operation of a divina-
tory instinct for truth,"[1] evidently believed that the work is effective
as drama because it is accurate as history. Whatever his own protestations to the contrary, his interpretation of the Maid's career is at least
as one-sided, both in its anti-clericalism and its "Protestant" individualism, as either Twain's or France's. Much of it, including specifically his claim that she got a fair trial, is outrageously anti-historical.

Yet, as he has reminded us in connection with the Eden myth, "the
validity of a story is not the same as the occurrence of a fact."[2] In
defining the "validity" of the Joan legend, he did possess one real
advantage over both his skeptical predecessors: He had, unlike them,
an essentially religious confidence in the ability of man to work out his
own redemption. Largely because of that confidence he was able, in
spite of his antipathy to Christian supernaturalism, to approach the
career of a Christian saint without falling victim either to "the idolatrous romance that has grown up round her" or to "the belittling
skepticism that reacts against that romance."[3]

Shaw's optimism has irritated some of his critics who see it as being
out of step with the modern spirit. Robert Brustein, for instance, in
The Theatre of Revolt,[4] complains that "Shaw's need to believe in the
possibilities of redemption rob his drama of an essential artistic office:
the ruthless examination of all illusions, no matter how unpleasant."
And he adds, "The function of the artist is not to console, not to adopt
a 'responsible' pose, not to support 'optimism' or 'pessimism'—but to
reveal, relentlessly, the truth that lies in the heart of man and in the
heart of the universe" (p. 208). Yet Brustein's assertion that some of the
greatest works of art "have achieved greatness by exposing things
which *might* tempt us to shoot ourselves" betrays a fundamental

misconception of the nature of tragedy. The greatest tragic art is always affirmative: the sinking at the heart which it produces depends, in large part, upon an exalted conception of human potential. Indeed, Brustein concedes that one of the functions of tragedy is to elevate us "with the prospect of human courage and nobility in the face of a terrible reality" (p. 209).

Moreover, Brustein's position is unsound philosophically as well as critically. It fails to explain why "the ruthless examination of all illusions" should be regarded as desirable. After all, one of the most significant findings of modern psychology is that our love of truth is never wholly disinterested: it is rooted, as Shaw repeatedly emphasized, in our deepest personal needs. For the very reason that truth often is unattractive, the regard in which it has always been held has depended largely on the optimistic conviction that all knowledge is ultimately redemptive. "And ye shall know the truth," declares the Christ of the Gospels, "and the truth shall make you free."

Finally, Brustein is also mistaken in his notion that Shaw's optimism depended on a misguided faith in "the essentially philanthropic nature of man" (p. 207). If he, unlike Twain and France, refused to despair, it is not because he was less aware than they were that a good misanthropic argument may be offered for doing so. "Man gives every reason for his conduct save one," he permits his Don Juan to declare, ". . .and that one is his cowardice. Yet all his civilization is founded on his cowardice, on his abject tameness, which he calls his respectability" (3: 621-22).

Although men may sometimes despair from a sense of guilt (which, indeed, was Twain's case) and even from temperamental melancholy (which seems to have been France's), they very rarely despair merely from misanthropic conviction. Actually, by far the most common cause of despair, as Shaw frequently insisted, is not disillusionment, but fear. For fear, by making men "respectable," renders them inveterately selfish; and where there is neither faith nor love, there can be no hope.

Hence Shaw is entirely correct in denouncing our modern despair as a rationalization for cowardice. It seems apparent that, in resisting it, he relied much less on philanthropic bias than on personal courage. More clearly than any other writer of his age, he insisted that the only inherently religious qualities are courage and self-respect. For him the fact that we cannot be happy without those qualities was a source of vital insight not only into the nature of man but also into the nature of things. "This is the true joy in life," he once wrote, "the being used for a purpose recognized by yourself as a mighty one; the being thoroughly worn out before you are thrown on the scrap heap; the being a force of nature instead of a feverish selfish little clod of ailments and grievances complaining that the world will not devote itself to making you happy. And also the only real tragedy in life is the being used by personally-minded men for purposes which you recognize to be base."[5]

It would probably be impossible to verify these observations scientifically; they must be taken as an affirmation of faith. But to embrace that faith we do not need to believe either in God or in the Life Force. All we need is sufficient self-respect to turn our backs upon despair.

CONCLUSION:

JOAN'S LAST TRIAL

Who will bring to us a new faith? a new hope? a new charity?
France, *"Pourquoi sommes-nous tristes?"*

In the period during which Twain, France, and Shaw were at work on Joan of Arc she was also undergoing a last ecclesiastical trial: the one which led to her canonization in 1924. By comparing the Catholic view of her which emerged from that trial with the skeptical views presented in the works we have studied we can gain fresh insight into the values which were at stake in the reaction against Christian fundamentalism that characterized the post-Darwinian era.

The case was first formally presented before the Sacred Congregation of Rites in 1888. At that time the promoter, or "devil's advocate," who signed his name in Latin as "Augustinus Caprara," made a sharp distinction between saintly and secular ideals of heroism. Drawing a parallel between Joan and Columbus, he pointed out that both had made great sacrifices on behalf of the faith, the one in bringing the New World under the influence of the Cross, and the other in liberating her country and consecrating it to the King of Heaven. Both, moreover, had received for this heroism the general admiration of mankind. Yet even so, Caprara argued, the virtues of both had always been regarded as purely "political." No one hitherto had attributed to Joan, any more than to Columbus, that "heroic virtue" which the Church defines as the distinguishing characterisitc of the saints.[1]

It was on the premise that "heröic virtue" is essentially spiritual rather than secular that Caprara built his case. Before a servant of God can be canonized, his supporters must prove that he achieved during his lifetime a reputation for sanctity. Caprara conceded that Joan's reputation had been great, but he argued that it had depended altogether too exclusively upon her military prowess. "Not Christian, therefore, but military was that heroic virtue which so stirred hearts and minds," he maintained.[2] And fifteen years later his successor at the Vatican, Alexander Verde, made the same point even more succinctly: "Not her virtues but her exploits were the cause of her renown."[3]

These remarks go to the heart of the disagreement between skeptics and believers concerning the nature of heroic virtue. They raise a question which is fundamental here: what should we value most in our heroes, pious virtues or practical ones?

For Joan's defenders in 1888, Messers Aldobrandi and Minetti, the answer to this question was not in doubt. They responded to Caprara's attack on Joan's reputation for sanctity by declaring that even in her own time she was chiefly remarkable for her kindliness, her charity to the poor, her love of prayer, and her constancy in taking the sacraments.[4] In 1903 their successors at the Vatican actually drew from Joan's stunning success a lesson on the vanity of earthly capacity. "That in the face of such pressing difficulties," they argued, "the Maid should in four months time have overcome more people than Napoleon and have retired from battle a conqueror of scarcely less renown can only be ascribed to the glory of God who, in His inscrutable wisdom, 'hath chosen the weak things of the world to confound the things which are mighty.'"[5] They even reasoned that, given Joan's natural infirmities, her achievement proves that she must have been virtuous, since God does not render supernatural aid to those who are not.[6]

Our three skeptics were contemptuous of this attitude. France, to be sure, agreed with the Maid's Catholic supporters that she was more distinguished for Christian piety than for natural ability. But since he did not share their faith in divine providence, he could reconcile this view of her with her amazing success only by supposing that she had been manipulated by men who were clever enough to be able to compensate for her own incapacity. "A great deal of art," he remarks in this connection, "and even a bit of chicanery, is always indispensable in gaining credit for innocence" (15:67). Shaw's Joan is so totally self-reliant that even the members of her own party accuse her of presumption: in Dunois's phrase, "she thinks she has God in her pocket" (2: 379). And Twain's attitude is expressed in his condemnation of the tribunal which the Dauphin established at Poitiers to inquire into the Maid's credentials as a messenger of God. "The rats were devouring the house," he makes De Conte complain, "but instead of examining the cat's teeth and claws they only concerned themselves to find out if it was a holy cat. If it was a pious cat, a moral cat, all right, never mind about the other capacities, they were of no consequence" (WMT 17: 160).

On similar grounds, Twain, France, and Shaw differed from the Maid's Catholic supporters in the stance they adopted toward the voices. In 1888 Caprara insisted that Joan's defense must prove that her saints had really come from God, arguing that her claim to divine inspiration could not otherwise be verified.[7] By contrast, the question on which our skeptics base their judgment of those saints is whether they gave her sensible advice.

Naturally, their answers to that question vary with their opinions of the imagination as a source of enlightenment. Both Twain and France find fault with the voices for being either uninformative or misleading. Shaw argues that their counsel, being a reflection of Joan's common sense, was actually quite sound. The common assumption underlying both views, however, is that in the absence of supernatural aids the hero must be realistic and practical. Knowledge of divine revelation cannot help him. What he needs is knowledge of the world.

Further, in the absence of a divinely revealed law, the hero must be morally, as well as practically, intelligent. He must have better values than his fellows, and he must refer his conduct to those values rather than to an abstract moral code. In 1888 Caprara quoted from one skeptic historian a passage which, while sympathetically intended, was damaging to the Maid from a Catholic point of view:

> I venture to say (so Quicherat) that she did not always respond truthfully to the question of her judges. When all that was at issue was her own person her response was characterized by that irresistible frankness to which I have just finished paying tribute; she avowed and affirmed at the risk of a thousand deaths. But if the demand revealed the slightest tendency toward an accusation that might fall on someone else, in that case she became evasive, she hesitated, she concealed her thought, and if further pressed, she dissembled.[8]

In denying that such mendacity may be excused by the generosity of its motive, the Church is guided by its mysticism. Since this world is merely a preparation for the next, it holds, the proper end of virtuous conduct must be not to secure worldly benefit even for others but entirely to fulfill the will of God. In 1888 Caprara explained what the Church understands by *heroic virtue*: that "it in fact reserves its highest and most exalted honors to those outstanding moral virtues which pertain to the eternal salvation of souls . . ."[9] In a preliminary brief presented in 1874, Giambattista Minetti completed a lengthy account of Joan's life and character by denouncing those whose love for the land of their fathers makes them, in his phrase, "unmindful of the kingdom of their heavenly father." Joan's elevation, he argued, would tend to counteract that sort of patriotism which "thrives without faith or religion and even provides an excuse for crimes."[10]

The skeptic, of course, recognizes no such transcendent allegiance. Hence his hero is a pragmatist. Just as he places his faith not in God but in himself, so also he places his hope not in a future life but in a better world. Consequently, he devotes all his energies to institutional reform; and being morally more intelligent than his fellows, he is likely to seem unscrupulous to them in the means which he uses to achieve such reform. In Twain, Joan not only sacrifices "her best self, that is, her truthfulness," to a patriotic purpose but she also justifies this course by a moral argument which her companions are too obtuse to comprehend. "Her saying had seemed shallow," De Conte declares in a canceled passage in the manuscript, "but that was because *we* were shallow; it was deep."[11] Shaw, going even further than Twain, claims that her moral originality put her so far in advance of the conventional ethics of her time that she was driven to become a heretic in order to assert the rights of the individual conscience against institutionalized morality.

Of our three skeptics, then, only France claims that Joan was lacking in moral intelligence, and his views on the subject have more in common with those of the others than is immediately apparent. In "Virtue in France" he declares, "Virtue is not an innocent. . . . It knows how, at need, to plunge with sublime impurity into all miseries in order to solace them, into all vices in order to redeem them. It knows the nature of the great human task, and that it is sometimes necessary to soil one's hands" (6:294). If, unlike Twain and Shaw, France denies such knowledge to Joan, he also indicates that it made her the ready dupe of unscrupulous opportunists.

The Church, however, refuses to approve the sacrifice of innocence to any earthly objective, however generous. Rejecting the pragmatic position taken by our skeptics, it holds that worldly success cannot be made a criterion of moral worth since, in the corrupt and uncertain condition of human affairs, such success does not always result from virtuous conduct. In 1888 Caprara argued that Joan's mission cannot really have been of God since she failed in her stated objectives of freeing the Duke of Orleans and driving the English out of France. The Maid's defense retorted that the failure of a sacred mission may be the fault not of the emissary but of those to whom he has been sent. If Joan's purpose was frustrated, they argued, it was because Charles VII too often heeded those of his counsellors who, unlike her, preferred to negotiate rather than fight. John the Baptist himself, they pointed out, had been prevented from fulfilling his goals by the wickedness and incredulity of his contemporaries.[12]

For the Church, then, the failure of the hero is not an index of the merit of his commitment, nor does it prove that his efforts have been wasted. But to those who cannot accept the Church's mystical view of this matter the very possibility of such failure raises a poignant ethical problem. "Her folly was wiser than wisdom itself," France declares in his preface, "for it was the folly of martyrdom, without which men have not established anything either great or useful in the world" (15:55). For Christians, however, martyrdom is more than a manifestation of the desire to establish the Kingdom of God on earth; it is also irrefragable proof that the martyr's love for God was greater than his love for the things of this world. To deprive his sacrifice of this mystic significance is apparently to make its merit depend upon its results. And over these he can exercise only a limited control.

France's solution to this difficulty lies in his declaration that sacrifice is beautiful in itself and that its merit is therefore independent both of its results and of the worthiness of its goals. His answer to the question, What, if not God, is the proper object of martyrdom? appears to be that the object as such does not matter. But this response is neither satisfying nor candid: it obviously matters to the martyr; it does not matter to France because he cannot imagine himself in the martyr's place. In fact, his genuine conviction appears to be that it is better to avoid martyrdom at all costs. In an essay for the *Temps*, where he describes martyrdom as a proof of fanaticism, he praises Rabelais for having avoided it.[13]

Moreover, as Shaw points out, the glorification of sacrifice for its own sake is ethically unsound, since it encourages people to sacrifice both themselves and others unnecessarily. France's claim in "Le Cavalier Miserey" that sacrifice is beautiful even when involuntary suggests that even for him its beauty was chiefly aesthetic rather than moral.[14] At any rate, his account of the Maid's death is far from edifying.

Shaw's treatment of this question is much more successful. Like Twain, he passes over the Catholic ideals of *caritate in deo* and *caritate in proximis* and represents Joan as having accepted martyrdom in response to an enlightened self-love. Impelled by a disinterested impulse of self-respect, he suggests, even the materialist can rise above material desires. Moreover, this idea can also be defended on pragmatic grounds, since it is only through confidence in his own intuitions that the hero can overcome the resistance which conventional people make toward revolutionary attempts at improving their lot.

Thus, like the Catholic hero's faith in God, the skeptic hero's faith in himself is at once the ground of his confidence in the future and the justification for his commitment. Perfecting himself in self-affirmation rather than in self-denial, he, unlike his Christian counterpart, makes a merit of personal pride. In the minutes of Joan's trial at Rouen, beside a passage which records one of her many defiant refusals to submit to the authority of the Church Militant, the scribe Manchon disapprovingly scrawled *"superba responsio!"* "Yes," Twain makes De Conte agree, "it was just that. For this 'superb answer' came from the lips of a girl of nineteen with death and hell staring her in the face."[15]

APPENDIX

MARK TWAIN'S BARGAIN WITH SATAN

In life, as in fiction, we feel intuitively or try to guess essential features of the unconscious character from the details of conscious self-characterization.
Reik, *The Compulsion to Confess*

Show freely to the world, if not your worst, yet some trait by which the worst may be inferred.
Hawthorne, *The Scarlet Letter*

My argument that Mark Twain once stole some money must begin with a concession; obviously I cannot claim to have discovered anything which could be used to convict him in court. Any evidence that he ever committed a serious crime must perforce be circumstantial. Presumably no one actually saw him do it, and he had the most compelling of motives for keeping it concealed. But a well-known maxim in psychology is that those whose consciences are burdened by a crime will normally be driven by a subconscious desire for punishment which will often impel them either to confess it or to hint ways by which it may be discovered. If that is the case here, then it should be possible to uncover some hints in Twain's writings.

That Twain was in fact affected by what Theodore Reik calls "the compulsion to confess" seems clear from certain remarks which he made about his autobiography. According to Paine, he originally was deeply concerned that "his deeds and misdeeds, even his moods and inmost thoughts, should be truly set down" (MTB, p. 674). Presumably in order to facilitate such frankness, he directed that the work was not to be published until after his death (MTA 1: xv). But "he confessed freely that he lacked the courage, even the actual ability, to pen the words that would lay his soul bare. . ." (MTB, pp. 674-75). "I have been dictating this autobiography of mine daily for three months," he declared in 1906. "I have thought of fifteen hundred or two thousand incidents in my life which I am ashamed of, but I have not gotten one of them to consent to go on paper yet. I think that that stock will still be complete and unimpaired when I finish this autobiography, if I ever finish it. I believe that if I should put in all those incidents I would be sure to strike them out when I came to revise this book" (MTA 2: 331).

Thus Twain was prevented, presumably by his fear of public disgrace, from unburdening his conscience openly. "Perhaps," he declares in "What Is Man?," "there is something that [man]loves *more* than he loves peace—*the approval of his neighbors and the public.* And perhaps there is something which he dreads more than he dreads pain—the *disapproval* of his neighbors and the public" (WIM, p. 137). But though he proved to be incapable of making a direct confession, the possibility remained open to him of making an indirect one through his fiction. And that idea seems, in fact, to have exerted a powerful hold upon his imagination.

That, at least, is clearly inferred from *Which Was It?*, an unfinished novel on which Twain worked intermittently from 1899 to 1903. The protagonist of that work, as DeVoto has pointed out, resembles Twain in a number of ways.[1] Two ways, not mentioned by DeVoto, are nonetheless important to our discussion. Like Twain, the protagonist decides to write an autobiographical narrative "for the easement it may give to look myself in the face and confess whither I have lately drifted, and what I am become!" And like Twain, he encounters intense psychological resistance in this effort. To overcome this resistance, he makes use of a striking narrative device:

> But I cannot do it in the first person; I must spare myself that shame; *must* is the right word; I could not say in the first person the things I ought to say, even if I tried. I could not say "*I* did such and such things;" it would revolt me, and the pen would refuse. No, I will write as if it were a literary tale, a history, a romance—a tale I am telling about another man, a man who is nothing to me, and whose weak and capricious character I may freely turn inside out and expose, without the sense of being personally under the knife. I will make of myself a stranger, and say "George Harrison did so and so."
>
> In the hope and belief that by the protection of this device I shall be enabled to frankly tell everything just as it happened, I will now begin. [WWD, p. 183]

Which Was It?, then, is a confessional "autobiography" written by an allegedly unknown author whom we nonetheless know to be Twain. If Twain did commit a serious crime, we may reasonably expect to learn something about it there.

That point of the work is spelled out early by one Sol Bailey—a so-called Idiot Philosopher who functions throughout the narrative as a mouthpiece for Twain's determinist views. At an inquest in which an act of homicide committed by George Harrison is actually blamed on a friend and benefactor of his, Bailey tortures Harrison's conscience by remarking that every man is morally a murderer, including Harrison himself. "To be a murderer in your heart," he asks, "and only saved from committing it by an accident of circumstance, what is that? It is murder just the same, isn't it? Of course. It is no merit of *yours* that you didn't do the deed. You are all murderers here, every one. . . . But if either of you here shall ever have that experience and kill a man, *that* lesson will stick and stay; you can never be caught out again by the passion of hate; grief and remorse will protect you, never again will you shed blood" (WWD, p. 280).

The claim made here that any man will fall if tempted beyond his "limit" is a common one in Twain's work; and his frequent and urgent insistence on it suggests that he must at some time have learned by experience what his own "limit" was. Even more revealing, however, is the point made at the end of the passage: that any man who has committed a notable crime will be prevented by his remorse from ever offending in the same way again. This is patently false: it depends on the man. Here again Twain is obviously relying on experience, and the compelling force with which he dramatizes the idea suggests that his own remorse must have been very great indeed.[2]

The logical implication of Twain's idea is that in his case also we have only a single offense to look for. This conclusion, by good fortune, is borne out by a rather slight but extremely significant piece of direct biographical evidence. In a short untitled sketch which Twain wrote in 1898, and which DeVoto called "Something about Repentance," he argues that men will normally repent a misdeed with much less bitterness than a good deed which has been ungraciously received. Twain remarks, "In my time I have done eleven good deeds. I remember all of them; four of them with crystal clearness. These four I repent of whenever I think of them—and that is not seldomer than fifty-two times a year. I repent of them in the same old original furious way, undiminished, always. If I wake up, away in the night, they are there, waiting and ready; and they keep me company till the morning. I have not committed any sin that has lasted me like this, *save one*; and I have not repented of any sin with the unmodifying earnestness and sincerity with which I have repented of these four gracious and beautiful good deeds" (WIM, p. 91; my emphasis).

What was the nature of that "sin" which, as Twain implies, stood "waiting and ready" to keep him company when he woke in the middle of the night? George Harrison is far from being the only character in *Which Was It?* who is tempted beyond his "limit." Another is a certain Mrs. Millikan, who, in her young womanhood, had succeeded in amassing a fortune from the poor by inducing them to participate in a fraudulent investment scheme. When she confesses this crime to her son, he responds with a series of rationalizations:

> Where you fell many would have fallen—good people, too, and primarily sound at heart. Bitter poverty and misery, then stupendous temptation and opportunity—why, if Sol Bailey is right, the fall was substantially certain. He says it's Circumstances, Temptation and Opportunity—this tremendous trinity—that makes criminals, not native wickedness. He says we all have our limit, and he wouldn't even trust George Harrison if circumstance, temptation and opportunity fell together and caught him behind his limit. [WWD, p. 337]

The phrase "bitter poverty and misery" points to the most significant "circumstance" which is shared in common by the cases of both George Harrison and Mrs. Millikan. "The lack of money is the root of all evil," Twain wrote in his notebook in 1905;[3] indeed, from *Huckleberry Finn* to "The Man That Corrupted Hadleyburg," that moral is confirmed in nearly all his major works. Temptation in Twain is virtually synonymous with the immediate need for cash.

We have therefore to look for a crime motivated by avarice, committed under straitened circumstances. It is inconceivable that Twain would have risked his international reputation by committing such a crime at a time when he possessed in his pen an extremely effective means of retrieving financial setback. Such an incident can only have occurred, then, while he was still an unestablished young man. This inference too is confirmed by independent evidence. In his autobiography Twain remarked that Susy died at an ideal age, since at twenty-four "the risks begin; responsibility comes, and with it the cares, the sorrows, and the inevitable tragedy" (MTA 2: 146). Clearly, this suggests that Twain's "inevitable tragedy" must have occurred early, and in fact, by 1858 he had come to describe himself as being one of the damned.[4]

Our task, then, is to discover in Twain's early years a point at which Circumstances, Temptation, and Opportunity "come together." The episode involving the fifty-dollar bank note appears to fit these conditions perfectly. As Twain describes it in "The Turning Point of My

Life," the episode occurred to a penniless, insecure, and highly unstable young man, who was clearly dissatisfied with his lot in life, and whose imagination had lately been inflamed by dreams both of great wealth and of romantic adventure in distant lands. The effect of these "circumstances" was reenforced by what he characterizes as one of his temperamental peculiarities. "By temperament," he explains, "I was the kind of person that *does* things. Does them, and reflects afterwards. . . . I have been punished many and many a time, and bitterly, for doing things first and reflecting afterward, but these tortures have been of no value to me . . ." (WIM, pp. 460-61). If I am right, Twain was indeed cruelly punished for the constitutional rashness which he displayed upon this occasion.

In any case, his claim that he discovered fifty dollars in the wind is wildly implausible. Even Paine concedes that it would be unacceptable in fiction, and we are not therefore obliged to conclude as Paine does that "fact has a smaller regard for the credibilities" (MTB, p. 110). The sum involved was equivalent, in current purchasing power, to some four hundred dollars. People do not "find" that kind of money. Nor do they leave it lying about for the wind to take. As a principle of historical verification, the claim that truth is stranger than fiction is irresponsible. If we are to believe something we would not accept in fiction, we must have hard evidence for it; and we have nothing harder in this case than the word of a neurotic, guilt-ridden old man uttered fifty years after the event.

Nor, in my view, did Twain expect his family to believe that story. On his way to South America he stopped over in Cincinnati, where, according to Paine, he remained from November until April (MTB, pp. 112-14). No one to my knowledge has yet accounted for this delay of five months in the fulfillment of a dream which filled Twain's imagination. Certainly such hesitation does not accord well with the sort of temperament which "does things . . . and reflects afterward." Twain had no need of more money; indeed, he seems to have left Cincinnati with less.[5] But he had to account to his mother for having any at all. And for that he needed to remain long enough in a strange city to be able to pretend that he had earned it.

Hence the fact that the period of Twain's stay in Cincinnati is by all odds the most poorly documented in his adult life.[6] He was lying low. And hence also the fact that he delayed for fifty years before reporting the striking and important incident of the banknote to his reading public. He had to wait until everyone who was familiar with his original story had died.[7]

"The Turning Point of My Life" was composed in response to an invitation from *Harper's Bazaar* to write about "the change in my life's course which introduced what must be regarded by me as the most *important* condition of my career" (WIM, p. 455). Since the offer came at a time when Twain was dying of angina pectoris, it must surely have struck him that here was an all but irresistible occasion for indirect confession.[8] "An autobiography," he had written to Howells two years earlier, "is the truest of all books; for while it inevitably consists mainly of extinctions of the truth, shirkings of the truth, partial revealments of the truth, with hardly an instance of plain straight truth, the remorseless truth *is* there, between the lines, where the author-cat is raking dust upon it which hides from the disinterested spectator neither it nor its smell. . .the result being that the reader knows the author in spite of his wily diligences."[9] Apart from the desire to reveal such truth "between the lines," it is difficult to understand why Twain should have referred to the banknote incident at all in "The Turning Point of My Life." As he describes it, that incident bears no evident relation to any of the major themes of his work. His account of the chain of circumstances which allegedly ties it to the beginning of his literary career is far from convincing.

That the intent of the essay is indeed confessional is confirmed by "The Parable of Two Apples," a short sketch with which Twain had begun the original draft. The two apples, of course, are the "good apple" and "bad apple" familiar to all Americans from their grade-school discipline. Their careers are similar to those of the "good little boy" and the "bad little boy" who figure in two of Twain's most popular short stories: the bad one prospers, and the good one comes to grief. In this case, however, these results are realized only after the two have passed, figuratively speaking, into the grave. For the point of the sketch is that men are good or bad not by choice but by force of circumstances and that it would therefore be no more arbitrary of Providence to reward the wicked and punish the virtuous than to do the reverse. Since Twain was actually dying at this time, it would be difficult not to see in this frivolous little parody of divine election and reprobation the wish-fulfilling fantasy of a guilt-ridden old man; this perception renders its relation to the subject of the essay as a whole startlingly clear. Here, as in "What Is Man?" Twain's covert motive in advancing his determinist thesis is to deny his own responsibility. And in this case he is denying responsibility for precisely "the change in my life's course which introduced what must be regarded by me as the most *important* condition of my career." In other words, the same "Circumstance" that made Twain an artist also made him a "bad apple."

This idea, moreover, is confirmed in *Which Was It?* In the introductory "frame" to that work, Allison Harrison, George's wife, writes of him, "I think he is literary in his make, indeed I feel sure of it. . .But he has never had to work for his living, and so he is easy-going and indolent, and has never had any troubles or sorrows or calamities to rouse up the literary fires that are slumbering in him and make them burst their bonds and find expression; therefore they can't seem to get started, lacking that impulse, do what I may to push him and pester him and persuade him to a trial of his gift. He only laughs and says 'fetch on your calamities, and I'm your man. . .' " (WWD, p. 179).

Since Twain was a writer, these remarks about the relation of personal suffering to the creative process presumably have a personal reference. We know that while he was still at Keokuk, shortly before the bank-note episode, he was told by a friend that he was too lazy ever to write a book (MTB, p. 107). Is it not significant, then, that when his "easy-going and indolent" protagonist does resolve to write one, he should be impelled by the remorse occasioned through the theft of money?

One advantage to the view that it was Twain's "fall" that made him a writer is that it provides a natural answer to the most challenging of the questions posed by Van Wyck Brooks. Twain contends in "What Is Man?" that even the greatest artist is a mere machine who can only reproduce without creating, and who is therefore not entitled to praise for the success of his work. Brooks asks, "But is it possible for a creative mind to find 'contentment' in denying the possibility of creation. . . ? Certainly it could not have afforded Mark Twain any pleasure to feel that he was 'entitled to no personal merit' for what he had done, for what he had achieved in life. . . ."[10] Brooks fails to recognize, however, that Twain, like Faust, had come to associate his power with his guilt.

Once we accept this conclusion it can be seen to throw a brilliant light on virtually the whole of Twain's serious creative output. "To me," he explained in "The Turning Point of My Life", "the most important feature of my life is its literary feature." Anyone who is familiar with the decisive role played in Twain's work by the theme of the fall and the related themes of guilt and retribution will immediately recognize that even from the literary point of view Twain's own "fall" must surely have been the "turning point" of his life. Indeed he implied as much when he declared, at the end of that essay, that in the Garden of Eden "the first link was forged of the chain that was ultimately to lead to the emptying of me into the literary guild" (WIM 463-64). For these words are surely more than a mere reaffirmation of the creed of determinism. They are also a veiled confession. And as such they provided Twain with what was perhaps the only insight through which, had he been spiritually capable of it, he might have achieved a measure of serenity.

To be sure, as he observed in the same place, it was clearly unjust of God to lay a trap for Adam and Eve into which they were predestined to fall, and thus bring suffering into the world. And it was equally unjust, as he seems to imply, that Joan of Arc, who would not have fallen, should nonetheless have been compelled to undergo such suffering in her own innocent person. But without suffering there can be no courage, and without courage—as her suffering itself demonstrates—there can be no love. So Twain, in the last year of his life, arrived on the threshold of that profound insight which is the burden of all tragic art: it is through the gateway of sin alone that man can enter into creation, and thus into fullness of being.

But Twain would have no part of a being that was rooted in sin and suffering. In a nihilism born of despair, he added, "What I cannot help wishing is, that Adam and Eve had been postponed, and Martin Luther and Joan of Arc put in their place. . . ." In that case, he concluded, "The apple would be intact to-day; there would be no human race; there would be no *you*; there would be no *me*. And the old, old, creation-dawn scheme of ultimately launching me into the literary guild would have been defeated" (WIM, p. 464).

NOTES

Notes to Part I, Chapter 1
Twain as Faust

1. The full title is *Personal Recollections of Joan of Arc, by the Sieur Louis de Conte (Her Page and Secretary), Freely Translated out of the Ancient French into Modern English from the Original Unpublished Manuscript in the National Archives of France by John François Alden*. Hereafter cited as *Joan of Arc*. It was written in slightly more than two years, from the winter of 1892-93 to January 1895. In *The Writings of Mark Twain*, definitive ed. 35 vols. (New York: Harper & Bros., 1922-25), vols. 17-18. Hereafter cited as WMT.
2. See Edward G. Rosenberger, "An Agnostic Hagiographer," in *Catholic World* 127 (Sept. 1928): 723.
3. Quoted in Albert Bigelow Paine, *Mark Twain: A Biography, The Personal and Literary Life of Samuel Langhorne Clemens* (New York: Harper & Bros., 1912), p. 1034. Hereafter cited as MTB.
4. *Mark Twain's Correspondence with Henry Huttleston Rogers, 1893-1909*, ed. Lewis Leary (Berkeley: Univ. of Calif. Press, 1969), p. 125.
5. Notebook 32, January 7, 1898 to July 18, 1899, typescript p. 28. In Mark Twain Papers, University of California at Berkeley. Hereafter cited as MTP.
6. *What Is Man? and Other Philosophical Writings*, ed. Paul Baender (Berkeley: Univ. of Calif. Press: 1973), pp. 128-31. Hereafter cited as WIM. The original draft of "What Is Man?" was not actually written until 1898, three years after the completion of *Joan of Arc*; but according to Paine it developed from an address called "What Is Happiness" which Twain had delivered to the Monday Evening Club, Hartford, February 1883. See MTB, pp. 743, 1321n.
7. WMT 22: 376-79. Written in 1899, "Saint Joan of Arc" was originally intended as the introduction to an English translation of the trial records. Twain recalled the manuscript after the editor, T. Douglas Murray, made some unsolicited emendations.
8. In "Saint Joan of Arc," Twain writes, "All the rules fail in this girl's case. In the world's history she stands alone—quite alone" (WMT 22: 378). In the so-called Translator's Preface to *Joan of Arc* he declares, "When we reflect that her century was the brutalest, the wickedest, the rottenest in history since the darkest ages, we are lost in wonder at the miracle of such a product from such a soil" (WMT 17: xxi).
9. Apparently written in 1899, two years after the completion of *Joan of Arc* and two years before the composition of "Saint Joan of Arc." It is cited in *Following the Equator*, WMT 20: 137.
10. For Twain's hostility to God, see "Concerning the Character of the Real God," an autobiographical dictation made on June 23, 1906, and published by Charles Neider as the fourth of five "Reflections on Religion" in *The Hudson Review* 16 (Autumn, 1963): 343-49. For his need for atonement, see esp. the autobiographical dictation, Feb. 2, 1906, in *Mark Twain's Autobiography*, ed. Albert Bigelow Paine, 2 vols. (New York: Collier & Son, 1925), 2: 37-39. Hereafter cited as MTA.

11. *The Tragicall History of the Life and Death of Doctor Faustus* 1. 1. 45-49.

12. *Faust* 1, 762-84. In Thomas Mann's *Doctor Faustus* the Faust figure, Adrian Leverkuhn, chooses to spend most of his adult career in a place that strikingly resembles his childhood home at Buchel. Mann's narrator, Serenus Zeitblom, finds the motives for this decision both obscure and unsettling.

13. Freud, "A Neurosis of Demonical Possession in the Seventeenth Century," in *Studies in Parapsychology*, ed. Philip Rieff. (New York: Crowell-Collier, 1963), pp. 91-92. Hereafter cited as NDP.

14. WMT 24: 326-28 (written 1902).

15. See Brooks, *The Ordeal of Mark Twain* (London: Heinemann, 1922), chap. 3.

16. In *Mark Twain's Fables of Man*, ed. John S. Tuckey (Berkeley: Univ. of Calif. Press, 1972), p. 165 (written 1905-1906). Hereafter cited as MTFM.

17. WIM, pp. 99-100 (written 1902).

18. WMT 22: 276-77 (written 1899).

19. WMT 29: 326-38 (written 1904).

20. WIM, pp. 459-61 (written 1909-1910).

21. My reasons are discussed in the appendix.

22. Discussed in appendix.

23. "The Dervish and the Offensive Stranger," WMT 29: 310 (written 1902).

24. In *Mark Twain's Which Was the Dream? and Other Symbolic Writings of the Later Years* (Berkeley: Univ. of Calif. Press, 1967), p. 234 (written 1899-1903). Hereafter cited as WWD.

25. In the autobiographical dictation, March 9, 1906, he claimed that he nearly drowned on eight separate occasions. See *Mark Twain's Autobiography*, ed. Albert Bigelow Paine, 2 vols. (New York: Collier & Son, 1925), 2: 184-85. Hereafter cited as MTA.

26. WIM, p. 458. He gives his age here as twelve; but in the autobiographical dictation for March 16, 1906, he claims that he was only ten, and this has been confirmed by Dixon Wecter. See his *Sam Clemens of Hannibal* (Boston: Houghton Mifflin, 1952), p. 297n3. The account betrays both the longing for death which prompted Twain's action and the narcissistic need which it was intended to gratify.

27. In later years, Twain spoke frequently of the fear of divine retribution aroused in him by his training. See MTA 1: 130-35; 2: 175-76; and *Life on the Mississippi*, chap. 54. He ultimately scoffed at the idea of such retribution, but the language he uses in doing so suggests that it persisted in his mind, even as a conscious persuasion, well into his maturity. See *Mark Twain in Eruption*, ed. Bernard DeVoto (New York: Harper & Bros., 1922), pp. 259-60.

28. *Mark Twain's Letters*, ed. Albert Bigelow Paine (New York: Harper & Bros., 1917), p. 40.

29. *Mark Twain and the Bible* (Lexington: Univ. of Kentucky Press, 1969), p. 6.

30. See esp. his discussion of "the honest man" in "What Is Man? (WIM, pp. 164-65). That Twain ultimately saw through this rationalization is apparent from a striking episode in *Which Was It?* See WWD, pp. 302, 305-9.

31. Which, pace Brooks, is also the covert moral of "The Man That Corrupted Hadleyburg" (written 1899). Beside an attack on Byron in Greville's *Journal*

of the Reigns of George IV and William IV he wrote, "But, dear sir, you are forgetting that what a man sees in the human race is merely himself in the deep and honest privacy of his own heart. Byron despised the race because he despised himself. I feel as Byron did, and for the same reason." MTB, p. 1539. See also *Mark Twain in Eruption*, p. xxix, and *The Autobiography of Mark Twain*, ed. Charles Neider (New York: Harper & Bros., 1959), p. 133.

32. Autobiographical dictation, Feb. 2, 1906, MTA, p. 34.

33. Mann, *Doctor Faustus*, trans. H. T. Lowe-Porter (New York: Alfred A. Knopf, 1948), p. 249.

34. *Mark Twain-Howells Letters: The Correspondence of Samuel L. Clemens and William Dean Howells* (Cambridge, Mass: Harvard Univ. Press, Belknap Press, 1960), p. 249.

35. MTFM, pp. 131-32 (apparently written in the summer of 1897).

36. It appears, for instance, in the suppressed "God" section of "What Is Man?" (1898), in "The Victims" (1900), in section 4 of "Reflections on Religion" (1906), in "The Private Secretary's Diary" (1907), in "Little Bessy" (1908-1909). Most of these works have recently been collected in MTFM. In every case the main thrust of Twain's hostility seems to be directed not so much against the cruelty of the doctrine as against the cruelty of God.

37. DeVoto, *Mark Twain at Work* (Cambridge, Mass.: Harvard Univ. Press, 1942), p. 115.

38. Autobiographical dictation, Feb. 26, 1906, MTA 2: 146.

39. Letter of March 25, 1887. Quoted in Wecter, *Sam Clemens of Hannibal*, p. 63.

40. See, for example, *Life on the Mississippi*, chap. 56.

41. Freud, *The Ego and the Id*, trans. Joan Riviere (New York: Norton Library, 1960), p. 42.

42. DeVoto, p. 116.

43. Notebook 32, June 22, 1897 to March 24, 1900, typescript p. 22, MTP.

44. WIM, p. 491. In the mid-nineties he wrote in his notebook that a God of his construction "would recognize in Himself the Author and Inventor of Sin, and Author and Inventor of the Vehicle and Appliances for its commission; and would place the whole responsibility where it would of right belong; upon Himself, the only Sinner." See *Mark Twain's Notebook*, ed. Albert Bigelow Paine (New York: Harper & Bros, 1935), p. 301. Hereafter cited as MTNB.

45. MTA 1: 263 (written in 1909).

46. Freud, *The Interpretation of Dreams*, trans. James Strachey, in *The Standard Edition of the Complete Psychological Works of Sigmund Freud*, 23 vols. (London: Hogarth Press, 1953), 5: 579-82.

47. See esp. "The Economic Problem in Masochism," in *General Psychological Theory: Papers on Metapsychology*, ed. Philip Rieff (New York: Crowell-Collier, 1963), pp. 199-200: "Now we know that the wish to be beaten by the father, which is so common, is closely connected with the wish to have some passive (feminine) sexual relations with him, and is only a regressive distortion of the latter . . . . In order to provoke punishment from this last parent substitute [fate] the masochist must do something inexpedient, act against his own interests, ruin the prospects which the real world offers him, and possibly destroy his own existence in the world of reality."

48. Several passages of *Joan of Arc* recall details from the brief biography of Twain's mother, "Jane Lampton Clemens," which he had written shortly after her death in 1890. According to Walter Blair, who edited a new edition of the work in 1969, it offers four instances of Jane Clemens's "largeness of heart": "her defense of Satan, her courageous defiance of 'a vicious devil of a Corsican . . . ,' her exploitation by pathetic cats, her consideration even of slaves." See *Mark Twain's Hannibal, Huck & Tom* (Berkeley: Univ. of Calif. Press, 1969), p. 42. All these matters are recalled in fictional form in Twain's account of the Maid's girlhood.

49. Twain's description of Joan as "deeply religious" in "Saint Joan of Arc" (WMT 22: 381) is an explanation for what he sees as an admirable fidelity to her voices. The desire for atonement which was reflected in this attitude, however, was largely escapist.

50. In a letter to his friend Joseph Twichell, dated Jan. 9, 1897, he wrote, "I am working, but it is for the sake of the work—the 'surcease of sorow' that is found there. I work all the days, and trouble vanishes away when I use that magic." *Mark Twain's Letters,* p. 641. The remark is revealing because it links the "magical" quality of Twain's later romances, characterized as they are by unrestrained flights of fantasy, with an escapist inclination rooted in private despair.

51. See esp. WMT 17: 54-60.

52. On the flyleaf of one of his sourcebooks, Mme. de Chabannes, *La Vierge lorraine Jeanne d'Arc,* Twain wrote, "Have several of her playmates come all the way, hoping somehow to save her—she glimpses them when she knows she is enroute to the stake & they don't—a little later they crowd in & get a glance—it is then the boy closes with Oh, my God!" (MTP).

Notes to Part I, Chapter 2
Joan as Visionary Prophet

1. The treatment of the professional liar Merlin in *A Connecticut Yankee* provides a case in point. For the Yankee's opinion of prophecy, see WMT 14: 270.

2. Chabannes, p. 54, MTP.

3. "Now consider these things. The French armies no longer existed. The French cause was standing still, our King was standing still, there was no hint that by and by the Constable Richemont would come forward and take up the great work of Joan of Arc and finish it. In face of all this, Joan made that prophecy—made it with perfect confidence—*and it came true*" (WMT 18: 162).

4. Which Twain indicates. See, for example, WMT 17: 140, 157.

5. The important statement of religious creed in which this passage appears was recently collected by Paul Baender as the first of "Three Statements of the Eighties." WIM, p. 56.

6. Antoine Ricard, *Jeanne d'Arc la Vénérable,* p. 228, MTP.

7. Rosenberger, p. 721.

8. See esp. MTA 2: 37-39.

9. Autobiographical dictation, June 20, 1906, in *The Hudson Review*, 16 (Autumn, 1963): 337.

10. Ricard, p. 23, MTP.

11. DeVoto, pp. 126-27.

12. In "Mental Telegraphy" (written 1891), Twain recounts a visionary experience of his own and suggests that such experiences may be explained in terms of the difficulty of distinguishing between dream and reality. WMT 22: 134-37.

13. In the autobiographical dictation, Jan. 13, 1906, Twain indicated that he took seriously the notion that "now and then . . . a dream which was prophetic turned up in the dreamer's mind" (MTA 1: 306-12).

14. Holograph MS, pp. 15-16, MTP.

15. "Then suddenly there was a great light! she lifted her head and caught it full in her swarthy face, which it transfigured with its white glory, as it did also all that place, and its marble pillars, and the frightened people . . . and so there they were, all kneeling, like that, with hands thrust forward or clasped, and they and the stately columns all awash in that unearthly splendor; and there where the magician had stood, stood 44 now, in his supernal beauty and his gracious youth; and it was from him that that flooding light came, for all his form was clothed in that immortal fire, and flashing like the sun." *No. 44, The Mysterious Stranger* (written 1902-1908), in *Mark Twain's Mysterious Stranger Manuscripts*, ed. William M. Gibson (Berkeley: Univ. of Calif. Press, 1969), p. 390. Hereafter cited as MSM.

16. See notebook entry Jan. 7, 1897, in MTNB, pp. 348-52.

17. MTNB, p. 395. The entry is dated Sept. 24, 1905. Livy died on June 4, 1904.

18. WIM, p. 483. In a letter dated Jan. 22, 1898, Twain had written to Howells, "It is my quarrel—that traps like that are set. Susy & Winnie given us, in miserable sport, & then taken away." *Mark Twain-Howells Letters*, p. 669. Winnie was Howells' daughter.

19. *No. 44, The Mysterious Stranger*, in MSM, pp. 404-5. "The Conclusion of the Book" was written in 1904.

Notes to Part I, Chapter 3
Joan as Woman of the People

1. O'Hagan, *Joan of Arc* (London: Kegan Paul, 1893), pp. 94-95. Twain's copy in MTP.

2. Autobiographical dictation, June 23, 1906, in *The Hudson Review* 16 (Autumn, 1963): 346.

3. Chabannes, p. 39, MTP; my translation. Twain's remark is headed "the Boy." He evidently intended to attribute it to De Conte.

4. From pp. 341-42 and 344 of the first of two batches of holograph manuscript. Page 343 was apparently discarded. My source for the MS. is a microfilm in MTP.

5. See Roger Salomon, *Twain and the Image of History* (New Haven: Yale Univ. Press, 1961), pp. 168-74, 187.

6. Chabannes, p. 25, MTP.

7. William Dean Howells, *My Mark Twain: Reminiscences and Criticisms,* ed. Marilyn Austin Baldwin (Baton Rouge: Louisiana State Univ. Press, 1967), p. 155.
8. See, for example, *Mark Twain in Eruption,* p. 211.
9. John 8: 32.

Notes to Part I, Chapter 4
Joan as Warrior Patriot

1. WMT 17: 117-18. Twain had originally written, "She would sacrifice herself—and her best self—that is, her truthfulness—to save her cause, but our attitude was to save both self and cause by deception." The passage is in the first of two batches of holograph MS., p. 179, MTP.
2. See, for example, "Travelling with a Reformer": "Lies told to injure a person, and lies told to profit yourself are not justifiable, but lies told to help another person, and lies told in the public interest—oh, well, that is quite another matter." WMT 22: 81 (written 1899). The same distinction is also made in "On the Decay of the Art of Lying," WMT 19: 364, and in "My First Lie and How I Got Out of It," WMT 23: 166-67.
3. The Paladin and the Dwarf. Concerning the latter, see Albert E. Stone, Jr., *"The Innocent Eye: Childhood in Mark Twain's Imagination* (New Haven: Yale Univ. Press, 1961), pp. 219-20.
4. Ricard, p. 183, MTP.
5. Michelet, p. 20, MTP.
6. *The North American Review,* 180 (Jan., 1905): 5.
7. In "The Czar's Soliloquy" (written 1905), Twain makes the czar observe that "nothing politically valuable was ever yet achieved *except* by violence." *North American Review,* 180 (March, 1905): 324.
8. See Notebook 29, January 26 to April 28, 1896, typescript p. 36, MTP, where Joan's "treatment" is adduced as evidence bearing on the topic question "Whether it were Desireable that the Human Race be Continued."

Notes to Part I, Chapter 5
Joan as Martyr to Human Responsibility

1. "Saint Joan of Arc," WMT 22: 374.
2. Notebook 29, January 26 to April 28, 1896, typescript p. 36, MTP.
3. When Mme. de Chabannes, for instance, claims that Joan's martyrdom was ordained as the means by which France might expiate the sin of creating a schism within the Church, Twain snorted, "According to these pious idiots that is just God's way—to burn & kill the innocent as a punishment of the guilty," pp. 156-57, MTP.
4. Notebook 29, January 26 to April 28, 1896, typescript p. 46, MTP.
5. *Mark Twain's Correspondence with Henry Huttleston Rogers,* p. 125.
6. Notebook 34, 1901, dated June 10, typescript p. 12, MTP.

7. Salomon, *Twain and the Image of History,* p. 187.

8. MTNB, p. 347 (written 1895).

9. WMT 24: 76. See also "On the Decay of the Art of Lying": "The man who speaks an injurious truth, lest his soul be not saved if he do otherwise, should reflect that that sort of soul is not strictly worth saying" (WMT 19: 364).

10. In 1892, during the composition of *Joan of Arc,* he spoke of hell to the actress Grace King: "I don't believe in it, but I'm afraid of it. When I wake up at night, I think of hell, and I am sure about going there." Quoted in Justin Kaplan, *Mr. Clemens and Mark Twain: A Biography* (New York: Simon and Schuster, 1966), p. 317.

11. Notebook 28A, May 15 to October 10, 1895, typescript pp. 21, 35-36, MTP. Quoted in Walter Blair, *Mark Twain & Huck Finn* (Berkeley: Univ. of Calif. Press, 1962), pp. 143-44.

Notes to Part I, Chapter 6
The Great Dark

1. See WWD, p. 131n. In *Mark Twain at Work* DeVoto remarks, "the Superintendent of Dreams exactly corresponds to God in *What Is Man?* Watch him become Satan," p. 122n.

2. See *Letters from the Earth,* ed. Bernard DeVoto (New York: Harper & Row, 1962), pp. 284-86.

Notes to Part II, Chapter 1
France and Naturalism

1. In *Oeuvres complètes illustrées de Anatole France,* 25 vols. (Paris: Calmann-Lévy, 1925-1935), vols. 15-16. Hereafter, unless otherwise indicated, all references to France's work cited by volume and page number are to this edition; my translation.

2. "Demain," in *La Vie littéraire,* 2d ser., 6:511; first printed in *Temps,* Aug. 5, 1888.

3. *Grand Dictionnaire Universel de XIXe Siècle,* s.v. "naturalisme."

4. *The Encyclopedia of Philosophy,* s.v. "naturalism."

5. Montaigne, *Complete Works: Essays, Travel Journal, Letters,* trans. Donald M. Frame (Stanford, Cal.: Stanford Univ. Press, 1958), p. 401. Montaigne was aware of, but unimpressed by, the heliocentric theory of Copernicus. It was not generally accepted in France until after the appearance in 1686 of Fontenelle's *Conversations on the Plurality of Worlds.*

6. In Voltaire, *Mélanges,* ed. Jacques van den-Heuvel (Paris: Gallimard, 1961), p. 158; my translation.

7. "Rêveries Astronomiques," in *La Vie littéraire,* 3d ser., 7:210; first published in *Temps,* Nov. 24, 1889. See also 9:418-19. For Montaigne, see *Complete Works,* p. 454.

8. *Le Jardin d' Epicure* (a series of philosophical reflections published together in 1895), 9:458.

9. *Les Opinions de M. Jérôme Coignard* (1893), 8:461.

10. From the preface to *La Vie Littéraire*, 2d ser. (published in 1890), 6:326.

11. In *La Vie littéraire*, 3d ser., 7:236; first printed in *Temps*, Jan 12, 1890. See also 7:355.

12. "M. Ernest Renan: historien des origines," in *La Vie littéraire*, 1st ser., 6: 287; 1st printed in *Temps*, Oct. 23, 1887.

13. In *La Vie littéraire*, 2d ser. 6: 662; first printed in *Temps*, Feb. 24, 1889.

14. Ernest Renan, *Histoire des origines de Christianisme*, 7 vols., vol. 1, *Vie de Jésus* (Paris: Calmann-Lévy, 1888), p. xxii; my translation. Hereafter cited as HOC.

15. For a detailed account of France's reaction to the Dreyfus affair, see Carter Jefferson, *Anatole France: The Politics of Skepticism* (New Brunswick: Rutgers Univ. Press, 1965), chap. 4.

16. Jean-Jacques Brousson, *Anatole France en Pantoufles* (Paris: Crès, 1924), p. 23; my translation. The remark was apparently made in 1904.

17. "Sur le miracle," in *Le Jardin d'Epicure*, 9:490; first printed as "A Propos de N.-D. de Lourdes," in *Echo de Paris*, May 1, 1894.

18. "Le R. [évérend] P. [ère] Didon et son livre sur Jésus-Christ," in *La Vie littéraire*, 4th ser., 7:487-88; first printed in *Temps*, Oct. 19, 1890. For Montaigne, see "It is Folly to Measure the True and False by Our Own Capacity," *Complete Works*, p. 133.

19. This, at all events, is the opinion of M. Bergeret, the Socrates of the dialogue on Joan of Arc which appears in *L'Orme du mail* (1897), chap. 10: "As for the child which the Maid brought back to life for the moment needed to administer baptism . . . I confine myself to reminding you that there was located near Domremy a [church dedicated to] Our Lady of the Aviots, whose specialty it was to reanimate for a few hours infants who were still born. I suspect that the memory of Our Lady of the Aviots was not foreign to the illusions under which Joan labored when she believed, at Lagny, that she had brought a newborn child back to life" (11: 104).

20. The "secret revelation" was that his birth was legitimate. For France's very different handling of this matter, see 15:258-59.

21. Compare this view with that expressed in Renan's introduction (HOC1: xcvi-xcvii). Renan would accept an act of resurrection as miraculous if it could be verified according to strict scientific criteria.

22. For recent Naturalist discussions of this problem, see Sidney Hook, "Naturalism and First Principles," in his *The Quest for Being* (New York, St. Martin's Press, 1961) pp. 172-95; and Ernest Nagel, "Naturalism Reconsidered," in *American Philosophy in the Twentieth Century*, ed. Paul Kurtz (New York: Macmillan, 1966), pp. 544-55.

23. Lang, *The Maid of France* (London: Longmans, 1908), p. 14.

24. Voltaire, *Lettres Philosophiques*, in *Mélanges*, p. 132; my translation.

25. *Complete Works*, p. 789.

26. "Le Miracle de Grand Saint Nicolas," in *Les Sept femmes de la Barbe-Bleu et autres contes merveilleux* (19:167-68); first printed in a supplement to the *New York Herald*, Paris ed., Dec. 13, 1908.

Notes to Part II, Chapter 2
Joan as Victim of Nervous Disorder

1. *La Rôtisserie de la Reine Pédauque* (1893), 8:181. France also makes this point in the preface to *Vie de Jeanne d'Arc* (15:50), and through his protagonist, M. Bergeret, in the dialogue on Joan of Arc which appears in *L'Orme du mail* (11:99 ff.). In both places he emphasizes that certain 17th-century Catholic scholars had denounced the legends of those saints as fables. "Is not that embarrassing, M. l'Abbé," asks M. Bergeret, "for those who believe that the voices of Joan of Arc came from heaven?" 11:103.

2. See his introduction to Freud and Breuer, *Studies on Hysteria*, in his *Works* 2:3-17. As Freud points out, Charcot recognized that some forms of hysteria are traumatically induced, but reasoned that in such cases the effect of the trauma had been to trigger an organic disorder in the nervous system.

3. As late as 1914 Freud complained that psychoanalysis was still badly misunderstood and misrepresented in France. See his *History of the Psychoanalytic Movement*, trans. Joan Riviere (New York: Norton Library, 1966), pp. 32-33.

4. "Les Fous dans la littérature," in *La Vie littéraire*, 1st ser., 6:169-71; first printed in *Temps*, June 19, 1887.

5. *Historical and Critical Dictionary: Selections*, ed. and trans. Richard H. Popkin (Indianapolis: Bobbs-Merrill, 1965), pp. 195-98 (article and remark B). France quotes from Bayle's Pyrrho entry in his 5Temps review of Victor Brochard's *Les Sceptiques Grecs*, 6:453.

6. Ibid., p. 204 (remark B and n.).

7. *Encyclopédie, ou Dictionnaire raisonné des sciences, des arts et des métiers* (Geneva: Pellet, 1777-79).

8. Preface to *La Vie littéraire*, 4th ser., 7:9; published 1891.

9. *Mélanges*, p. 176.

10. Walter Jackson Bate discusses this intellectual movement in his *Prefaces to Criticism* (Garden City, N.Y.: Doubleday, 1952), pp. 100-4.

11. Michelet, *Joan of Arc*, trans. Albert Guérard (Ann Arbor: Univ. of Michigan Press, 1957), p. 9.

12. *Les apôtres*, in HOC 2:13; my translation.

13. Paul Gsell, *Les Matinées de la Villa Said* (Paris: Grasset, 1922), pp. 77-78; my translation. In all quotations I have ignored Gsell's impressionistic paragraphing.

14. What he meant by applying the word *radiant* to Joan's saints can best be understood by examining his version of the Mystic Marriage of St. Catherine (*Vie de Jeanne d'Arc*,15:12). The passage is imbued with that sentimental glorification of medieval legend which characterized late 19th-century Aestheticism. To his friend Nicolas Segur, France once remarked, "As for me, I serenely and deliberately prefer legends to history. They are not more false. And flatteringly arranged by men who want to see themselves improved in them, they are more agreeable, more consoling, than reality." Segur, *Conversations avec Anatole France ou les mélancolies de*

l'intelligence (Paris: Fasquelle, 1925), p.112; my translation.

15. "Le R. P. Didon et son livre sur Jésus-Christ," 7:486.

16. "Her Voices," France observes at one point, "encouraged her uncertainty. They only showed her what she ought to do when she knew it herself" (16:27). At Domremy they told her to go to the Dauphin at Chinon but neglected to tell her how to go about it. "How was she to go into France? How was she to go among men at arms? The Voices that she listened to, as ignorant and as generous as she, revealed nothing to her but her soul and left her in a lamentable state of distress" (15:126).

17. A similar delusion of invincibility, France claims, contributed to her capture at Compiegne, 16:166-67.

18. "M. Leconte de Lisle à l'Académie française," in *La Vie littéraire*, 1st ser., 6: 97-98; first printed in *Temps*, Mar. 27, 1887.

19. In "Hypnotisme dans la littérature: Marfa," France remarks that he envies the scientist William Crookes his celebrated "visions" of Katie King: "And by way of consolation we tell ourselves that if we do not see her it is because we have too much good sense, but we flatter ourselves; it is in reality because we do not have enough imagination. It is from want of hope and faith; it is from want of virtue." *La Vie littéraire*, 1st ser., 6:113-14; first printed in *Temps*, Apr. 24, 1887.

20. "A propos du Journal des Goncourts," in *La Vie littéraire*, 1st ser., 6: 87; first printed in *Temps*, Mar. 20, 1887.

21. Gsell, *Les Matinées de la Villa Said*, p. 78.

22. For Renan, see HOC 1: ix.

23. "J'ai les doigts crochus du sceptique qui analyse." Nicholas Segur, *Dernières conversations avec Anatole France* (Paris: Fasquelle, 1927), pp. 176-77; my translation. The remark was made "bien après le mort de Mme. de C[aillavet]," France's patroness, that is, after Jan. 12, 1910.

24. "Mérimée," in *La Vie littéraire*, 2d ser. 6:383; first printed in *Temps*, Feb. 19, 1888.

Notes to Part II, Chapter 3
Joan as Tool of the Armagnac Clergy

1. "Sur Jeanne d'Arc," 7:244-45.

2. "Mysticisme et science," in *La Vie littéraire*, 4th ser., 7:233; first printed in *Temps*, Apr. 27, 1890.

3. See *Pierre Nozière*, 10:514, and *Vie de Jeanne d'Arc*, 16:451.

4. See *The New Catholic Encyclopedia*, s. v. "canonization of saints, history and procedure."

5. See also 15:36,122-24.

6. See also 15:145: "She could not by herself have discovered either the word or the concept: she had manifestly been indoctrinated by one of those clerics whose influence we have already discerned . . ."

7. *L'Orme du mail* is the first of a series of four novels collectively entitled *Histoire contemporaine*. The three chapters dealing with Mlle. Deniseau (11: 89-120) were first published serially in *Echo de Paris*, April and May, 1896.

8. Brousson, p. 202.

Notes to Part II, Chapter 4
Joan as Religious Fanatic

1. Abraham Edel, "Naturalism and Ethical Theory," in *Naturalism and the Human Spirit*, ed. Yervant H. Krikorian (New York: Columbia Univ. Press, 1944), p. 65.
2. *L'Avenir de la science: pensées de 1848* (Paris: Calmann-Lévy, n. d.), pp.125-26. For France's reaction to Renan's views on this subject, see *Le Jardin d'Epicure*, 9:420: "Renan abandoned himself freely and smilingly to the dream of a scientific morality. He had a faith in science which was almost unlimited. He believed that it would change the world, since it pierces mountains. I do not think, as he does, that it can make us Gods. To tell the truth, I scarcely want it to. I don't feel the makings of a god in me, however small. My weakness is dear to me. I cling to my imperfections as to my *raison d'être.*"
3. Quoted by Victor Brochard in *Les Sceptiques Grecs* (Paris: Vrin, 1969), p. 58; my translation. France reviewed the original edition of this book in "Sur le Scepticisme," *La Vie littéraire*, 2d ser., 6:446-54; first printed in *Temps*, May 22, 1888.
4. First published in *Echo de Paris*, March 19, 1896; reprinted in *Pierre Nozière*, 10:381.
5. Preface to *La Vie littéraire*, 6:5; published in 1888.
6. "Sérénus," in *La Vie littéraire*, 1st ser., 6:20-24; first printed in *Temps*, Dec. 12, 1886.
7. Segur, *Conversations avec Anatole France*, p. 197.
8. In *Essays in Pragmatism*, ed. Abury Castell (New York: Hafner, 1948), p. 104.
9. Compare Bayle: "In order to doubt one must have a certain measure of intelligence, which not everyone has. Nothing is more difficult than to doubt as one should. . . ." *Nouvelles Lettres*, quoted in Craig B. Bush, *Montaigne and Bayle: Variations on the Theme of Skepticism* (The Hague: Nijhoff, 1966), pp. 245-46; my translation.
10. From an address delivered March 4, 1900, at the inaugural celebration of the popular university "Le Reveil." In *Vers les temps meilleurs: trente ans de vie sociale*, ed. Claude Aveline, 3 vols. (Paris: Emile Paul, 1949), 1:38.
11. "Un nouveau Evangile: Jésus à Paris," a review of *Contes Chretiens: Le Baptême de Jésus ou les quatre dégrés de scepticisme* by T. de Wyzewa, in *La Vie littéraire*, 5th ser. (Paris: Calmann-Lévy, 1949), pp.218-19; first printed in *Temps*, July 17, 1892.

Notes to Part II, Chapter 5
Joan as Martyr to Superstititon

1. "La Vertu en France," in *La Vie littéraire*, 1st ser., 6:296; first printed in *Temps*, Oct. 30, 1887.
2. Voltaire, *Traité de métaphysique*, in *Mélanges*, p. 197.
3. Dewey, "Antinaturalism in Extremis," in Krikorian, pp.1-2.
4. *Historical and Critical Dictionary*, s.v. "Paulicians," remark E.

5. Speech delivered at the inaugural celebration of the popular university "Emancipation," Nov. 21, 1899. In *Vers les temps meilleurs*, 1:29.
6. *Mélanges*, p. 197.
7. Ibid., pp. 198-99: "'But,' they will tell me, 'in that case, it will only be with regard to us that there will be crime and virtue, moral good and moral evil; will there then be nothing that is good in itself and independently of man?' I would ask those who put this question if there be hot or cold, sweet or bitter, good smells or bad ones otherwise than with regard to us? . . . Our physical good and evil exist only with regard to us; why would our moral good and evil be in another case?"
8. See France's complaint in *L'Eglise et la république* (1905) that the doctrine of the monk "obliges him to join souls to his incomprehensible God, before joining them to each other through sympathy and pity." *Vers les temps meilleurs*, 2:40. For Voltaire, see, for example, *Traité sur la tolerance*, in *Mélanges*, p. 627.
9. *Complete Works*, p. 369.
10. *La Révolte des anges* (1914), 22:157.
11. See *The New Catholic Encyclopedia*, s.v. "martyrdom, theology of."
12. See Dewey, in Krikorian, pp. 6-7: "The interpretation put by Saint Thomas Aquinas (now the official philosopher of the Church) upon the Biblical injunction 'Love thy neighbor as thyself' is proof for the orthodox that since the love in question is love of an immortal and nonnatural soul, which can be saved only by acceptance of the creed of the Church and by sharing its sacraments, the injunction of Jesus is so far from having the meaning that would naturally be assigned to it that it expressly authorizes any and all means that may tend to save the soul from the tortures of hell."
13. "Pierre Lafitte," an address delivered in São Paulo, Brazil, in 1909, 17:309.

Notes to Part II, Chapter 6
How History Is Made

1. "Jeanne d'Arc et la Poesie," *La Vie littéraire*, 2d ser., 6:662; first printed in *Temps*, Feb. 24, 1889.
2. *Anatole France à la Bechellerie*, p. 249. "One recognizes those who are favored of God, my son," remarks M. Coignard in *Les Opinions de M. Jérôme Coignard*, "by this: that they are without intelligence; and my experience has been that the very lively intelligence that heaven has endowed me with has merely been a perpetual source of perils to my peace in this world and in the other" (8:413).
3. Michel Corday, *Anatole France d'après ses confidences et ses souvenirs* (Paris: Flamarion, 1927), p. 143; my translation. France also told Corday that the Maid was "une innocente—simplicissima" (p. 144). His acquaintance with Corday lasted from 1912 to 1924.
4. Letter read at a meeting of the National Association of Free-Thinkers, July 15, 1905. In *Vers les temps meilleurs*, 2:110.
5. "Pourquoi sommes-nous tristes?" in *La Vie littéraire*, 3d ser., 7:21-22; first printed in *Temps*, Mar. 31, 1889.

Notes to Part III, Chapter 1
Shaw and Vitalism

1. *Saint Joan*, in *Complete Plays with Prefaces*, 5 vols. (New York: Dodd-Mead, 1963), 2:263-431. Hereafter all references to Shaw's plays and prefaces are to this edition. *Saint Joan* was first produced in 1924, and its preface has same date.
2. Shaw was fond of quoting this phrase, which he claimed to have heard in conversation with Butler. See *The Religious Speeches of Bernard Shaw*, ed. Warren Sylvester Smith (New York: McGraw-Hill, 1963), pp. 13, 48, 75.
3. "The Religion of the Future," in *Religious Speeches*, p. 33, a speech delivered at a meeting of the Heretic's Society, May 29, 1911.
4. "Modern Religion I," in *Religious Speeches*, p. 48; prepared from a speech delivered at the New Reform Club in London, March 21, 1912.
5. See preface, 2:275-76.
6. "Modern Religion I," in *Religious Speeches*, p. 49.
7. In *The Adventures of the Black Girl in Her Search for God*, he contemptuously characterizes Jesus as "the conjuror." See also "Modern Religion I", in *Religious Speeches*, p. 47, and the preface to *Back to Methuselah* (1920), 2:xxxix-xl.
8. From an attack on G. K. Chesterton in "The Chesterbelloc: a Lampoon," in *The New Age*, Feb. 15, 1908; reprinted in *The Collected Works of Bernard Shaw*, Ayot St. Lawrence ed., 30 vols. (New York: William H. Wise, 1932), 29:80. Hereafter cited as *Works*.
9. *Religious Speeches*, pp. 6-7. Delivered in the City Temple, Nov. 22, 1906; first printed in *The Christian Commonwealth*, Nov. 29, 1906.
10. "A miracle, my friend, is an event which creates faith" (2:340).
11. *The Revolutionist's Handbook*, appended to *Man and Superman* (written 1901 and 1903), and attributed to John Tanner, the protagonist of that play, 3:693.

Notes to Part III, Chapter 2
Joan As Galtonic Visualizer

1. Galton (London, 1883), pp. 176-77. In the preface to *Saint Joan*, Shaw calls the Maid a "Galtonic visualizer" (2:280).
2. "All the popular religions in the world are made apprehensible by an array of legendary personages . . . . These are presented to the mind's eye in childhood; and the result is a hallucination which persists strongly throughout life when it has been well impressed . . . . And when, in the case of exceptionally imaginative persons . . . the hallucination extends from the mind's eye to the body's, the visionary sees Krishna or the Buddha or the Blessed Virgin or St. Catherine, as the case may be" (2:277).
3. Galton, pp. 164-72. Galton continues, "the spiritual discipline undergone for purpose of self-control and self-mortification have [sic] also the incidental effect of producing visions. It is to be expected that these should often

bear a close relation to the prevailing subjects of thought, and though they may be really no more than the products of one portion of the brain, which another portion of the brain is engaged in contemplating, they often, through error, receive a religious sanction" (p. 174).

4. "The Religion of the Future," in *Religious Speeches,* p. 34. See also "The Infancy of God," an essay apparently written in the twenties, in *Shaw on Religion,* ed. Warren Sylvester Smith (New York: Dodd-Mead, 1967), pp. 140-41.

5. *Religious Speeches,* p. 39.

6. *The Shrewsberry Edition of the Works of Samuel Butler,* ed. Henry Festing-Jones and A. T. Bartholomew, 20 vols. (London: Jonathan Cape, 1923-1926), 5:304-5. Hereafter cited as *Works.*

7. *Unconscious Memory,* in *Works,* 18:13-24.

8. *Back to Methuselah,* pt. 1. See discussion at end of this chapter.

9. Bergson, *Creative Evolution,* trans. Arthur Mitchell (New York: Henry Holt, 1911), p. 192. Butler presents this paradox more tersely in *Life and Habit:* "Thus a boy cannot really know how to swim till he can swim, but he cannot swim till he knows how to swim." *Works,* 4:240. For his solution, see *Evolution Old and New,* in *Works* 5:42-43.

10. Shaw may well have gotten this idea from William Blake. In his "There Is No Natural Religion I" Blake writes:

   V. Man's desires are limited by his perceptions, none can desire what he has not perceiv'd.
   VIM The desires & perceptions of man, untaught by any thing but organs of sense, must be limited to objects of sense.
   Conclusion. If it were not for the Poetic and Prophetic character the Philosophic & Experimental would soon be at the ratio of all things, & stand still, unable to do other than repeat the same dull round over again.

11. *Shaw on Theatre,* ed. E. J. West (New York: Hill & Wang, 1958), p. 116.

12. This conception of the imagination as the guiding force behind evolution seems to be Shaw's most distinctive contribution to Vitalist doctrine. Bergson also held that imagination arises in response to "a fundamental need of life", but Shaw's idea that it is "the beginning of creation" is entirely out of keeping with the anti-teleological cast of Bergson's thought. For Bergson's views on the evolutionary role of that faculty, see *The Two Sources of Morality and Religion,* trans. R. Ashley Audra and Cloudesley Brereton (New York: Henry Holt, 1935), pp. 109 ff., 184 ff.

13. See Michelet, *Joan of Arc,* p. 9.

14. Bergson, *Creative Evolution,* pp. 223-24.

15. Ibid., p. 224 ff.; see also pp. 30-33.

16. 6:63. Shaw's dramatization of the dispute between Kneller and Newton was inspired by William Hogarth's observation that, in Shaw's paraphrase, "the line of Nature is a curve"—a remark which, according to him, anticipated the Einsteinian theory that the universe is curvilinear. See "Religion and Science," in *Religious Speeches,* p. 86, an after-dinner speech delivered in honor of Albert Einstein, Oct. 28, 1930.

17. *The Adventures of the Black Girl in Her Search for God,* in *The Black Girl in*

Search of God and Some Lesser Tales (London: Constable, 1932), p. 3. Hereafter cited as *Black Girl.*

18. See, for example, the preface (written 1900) to *Three Plays for Puritans,* 3:xxxi-xxxiii.

19. Shaw makes this distinction in the preface to *Saint Joan:* "Criminal lunatic asylums are occupied largely by murderers who have obeyed voices . . . . By a medico-legal superstition it is held in our courts that criminals whose temptations present themselves under these illusions are not responsible for their actions, and must be treated as insane. But the seers of visions and the hearers of revelations are not always criminals. The inspirations and intuitions and unconsciously reasoned conclusions of genius sometimes assume similar illusions" (2:273). He seems, moreover, to have regarded the vision which appeared to St. Paul on the road to Damascus as peculiarly delusive. See the 1915 preface to *Androcles and the Lion,* 5:396.

20. Trans. E. F. J. Payne, 2 vols. (Indian Hills, Colo.: The Falcoln's Wing Press, 1958), 1:186-87.

21. In the "Don Juan in Hell" episode of *Man and Superman,* Don Juan remarks, "My dog's brain serves only my dog's purposes; but my brain labors at a knowledge which does nothing for me personally but makes my body bitter to me and my decay and death a calamity. Were I not possessed with a purpose beyond my own, I had better be a ploughman than a philosopher . . ." (3:645).

22. On the grounds that "temptation and inspiration mean the same thing." See n.5 above.

23. Shaw makes a similar point through the serpent's ambiguous description of the verb *to conceive* as "the word that means both the beginning in imagination and the end in creation" (2:10). For Shaw the double use of this verb is no mere linguistic accident; rather, it testifies to the persistence in verbal convention of truths which are no longer consciously recognized. See pt. 3, *The Tragedy of an Elderly Gentleman,* where Zoo tells the elderly gentleman that "thoughts die sooner than languages," and explains, "I understand your language; but I do not always understand your thought" (2:149).

Notes to Part III, Chapter 3
Joan As Vitalist Genius

1. *Shaw on Theatre,* p. 244.

2. "Joan of Arc—Heretic or Saint?" in the *Commonweal,* Nov. 2, 1934, p. 17. Another "instructed" Catholic, Pope Benedict XV, insisted on the injustice of Joan's trial in the very edict that made her a saint. For a translation of that edict, see Claire Marie Nicholson, *The Maid of Domremy: A Portrait of Joan of Arc* (New York: Exposition Press [1957]), pp. 91-92.

3. See *Saint Joan: A Screenplay by Bernard Shaw,* ed. Bernard F. Dukore (Seattle: Univ. of Washington Press, 1968), pp. 145-46, nn. to pp. 77, 99-101. Hereafter cited as *Screenplay.*

4. See also *Religious Speeches*, pp. 62-63.

5. "The New Theology," in *Religious Speeches,* p. 19.

6. He cautioned his French translators, Augustine and Henriette Hamon, that "heroic virtue" and "private revelations" are technical terms in theology, and advised them to ask a priest for the exact French equivalents. See *Sainte Jeanne,* typescript p. 133, margin, Academic Center Library, University of Texas, Austin.

7. A point made by her defense in the ecclesiastical trial which led to her canonization. See "Responsio ad Animadversiones," p. 2, art. 2, in *Positio Super Introductione Causae* (Rome: The Vatican Press, 1893).

8. See *Screenplay,* p. 147, nn. to pp.111, 112.

9. *Screenplay,* p. 143, n. to p.19; p. 146, n. to p.106.

10. In the ecclesiastical trial which led to Joan's canonization, her defense argued that "it is well known that because of his infinite truth miracles cannot be performed by God which should confirm a false opinion of the sanctity of any man." See also *The New Catholic Encyclopedia,* s.v. "canonization of saints, history and procedure."

11. *The Imitation of Christ,* trans. William Benham, in *The Harvard Classics,* 6:222.

12. *Screenplay,* p. 145, n. to p.79.

13. In the *The Devil's Disciple* we find:
    Judith *(sitting down helplessly)*: Is it of any use to pray, do you think, Tony?
    Anderson *(counting the money):* Pray! Can we pray Swindon's rope off Richard's neck?
    Judith: God may soften Major Swindon's heart.
    Anderson *(contemptuously, pocketing a handful of money):* Let him then. I am not God; and I must go to work another way.

14. *Black Girl,* p. 301.

15. First printed as a supplement to *The New Statesman,* Nov. 14, 1914; reprinted in *What I Really Wrote about the War,* in *Works* 21:100. In the filmscript Shaw has d'Alencon tell Joan, "You must learn when to be a saint and when to be a soldier; for you cannot be both at the same time" (*Screenplay,* pp. 61-62).

16. This ideal had appeared in Shaw's work by 1904. At the climax of *John Bull's Other Island,* Father Keegan, the protagonist, remarks of heaven, "In my dreams it is a country where the State is the Church and the Church is the people: three in one and one in three" (2:611).

17. Shaw apparently learned this from experience: "I was a coward until Marx made a Communist of me and gave me a faith," "Biographer's Blunders Corrected," in *Sixteen Self Sketches* (New York: Dodd Mead, 1949), p. 170.

18. *Screenplay,* p.143, n. to p.21. See also 2:329-30.

Notes to Part III, Chapter 4
Joan As Protestant

1. *Works,* 19:226-27; first printed in 1898.

2. *Works*, 19:186-87. At about the time he wrote *Saint Joan* Shaw made another objection to the practise of ruling people by imposing on their superstitions. In "The Infancy of God" he wrote, "We want intelligent obedience instead of idolatrous obedience, as that is our only guarantee against the abuse of power for the private ends of those whom we trust with it." *Shaw on Religion*, p. 136.
3. Marginal note in Shaw's handwriting on a letter from Martin H. Gildert of West Malvern, Worcester, dated Nov. 25, 1946. In the Academic Center Library, University of Texas, Austin.
4. See also the 1905 preface to *Major Barbara:* "The originality of Shakespeare's version [of Hamlet] lay in his taking the lunatic sympathetically and seriously, and thereby making an advance towards the eastern consciousness of the fact that lunacy may be inspiration in disguise, since a man who has more brains than his fellows necessarily appears as mad to them as one who has less" (1:300).
5. *Sainte Jeanne*, facing p. 13. Typescript in the Academic Center Library, University of Texas, Austin.
6. See, for example, *The Quintessence of Ibsenism*, in *Selected Non-Dramatic Writings*, ed. Dan H. Laurence (Boston: Houghton Mifflin, 1965), p.215n: "Those who give up materialism whilst clinging to rationalism generally either relapse into abject submission to the most paternal of the Churches, or are caught by the attempts, constantly renewed, of mystics to found a new faith by rationalizing on the hollowness of materialism. The hollowness has nothing in it; and if you have come to grief as a materialist by reasoning about something, you are not likely, as a mystic, to improve matters by reasoning about nothing."
7. "Postscript after Twenty-five Years" appended to the preface to *Back to Methuselah*, World Classics ed.; reprinted in *Complete Plays with Prefaces*, 2:ciii.
8. Preface (written 1933) to *On the Rocks*, 5:522.
9. "Jesus-Pilate Scene," 5:522.
10. For Shaw's pejorative use of the phrase "religion, law and order," see *The Perfect Wagnerite*, in *Works* 19:228.
11. The Catholic censor of Shaw's filmscript demanded that this line be cancelled, *Screenplay*, p. 146, n. to p. 104.
12. *The Quintessence of Ibsenism*, in *Selected Non-Dramatic Writings*, p. 213.
13. See, for example, "The Rejected Statement" (1909) in the preface to *The Shewing-Up of Blanco Posnet:* "Whatever is contrary to established manners and customs is immoral. An immoral act or doctrine is not necessarily a sinful one: on the contrary, every advance in thought and conduct is by definition immoral until it has converted the majority. For this reason it is of the most enormous importance that immorality should be protected jealously against the attacks of those who have no standard except the standard of custom, and who regard any attack on custom—that is on morals—as an attack on society, on religion, and on virtue" (5:191).
14. Preface to the 1907 edition of *The Sanity of Art*, in *Works* 19:301.
15. *Selected Non-Dramatic Writings*, p. 222.
16. *The Intelligent Woman's Guide to Socialism and Capitalism* (New York: Brentano's, 1928), p. 54.
17. At Kingsway Hall on Nov. 25, 1932, he began a lecture "In Praise of Guy

Fawkes" with the complaint: "For forty-eight years I have been addressing speeches to the Fabian Society and to other assemblies in this country. So far as I can make out, those speeches have not produced any effect whatever. In the course of them I have solved practically all the pressing questions of our time; but as they go on being propounded as insoluble just as if I had never existed, I have come to see at last that one of the most important things to be done in this country is to make public speaking a criminal offense." *Platform and Pulpit,* ed. Dan H. Laurence (New York: Hill & Wang, 1961), p. 235.

18. Shaw probably got this point from Anatole France. He seems not to have been aware of it before his reading of *Vie de Jeanne d'Arc* in 1924.

Notes to Part III, Chapter 5
Joan as Martyr to the Life Force

1. *Selected Non-Dramatic Writings,* pp. 216-17.

2. Significantly, Joan's military vocation fulfills this condition; see 2:280-82, 353.

3. *Selected Non-Dramatic Writings,* p. 217. In later editions Shaw weakened this to "the man's god is his own humanity"; see *Works* 19:26.

4. "The Only Hope of the World," a lecture given in Digswell Park, August 5, 1931, in *Platform and Pulpit,* p. 226.

5. See "The New Theology," in *Religious Speeches,* p. 17.

6. See "The Religion of the Future," in *Religious Speeches,* p. 34. For the identification of inspiration as the Holy Ghost, see esp. *The Revolutionist's Handbook,* 3:693.

7. The protagonist of "The Glimpse of Reality," a playlet written in 1909, undergoes a comparable conversion: "A priest said to me once, 'In your last hour everything will fall away from you except your religion.' But I have lived through my last hour; and my religion was the first thing that fell away from me" (4:742-43).

8. See *Luck, or Cunning?,* in *Works,* 8:112. See also Shaw's "Modern Religion II," a lecture delivered at the Hampstead Conservatoire, Nov. 13, 1919: "It is like a man saying, 'Where is the soul?' I always say to a materialist of that kind, 'can you tell me the difference between a living body and a dead one? Can you find out the life . . .? Why do I not crumble into my constituent chemicals?' None of these material people can tell me that." *Religious Speeches,* p. 76.

9. Quoted as it appears in the filmscript. Significantly, the Catholic censor cancelled the whole of it from "You think that life is nothing" to "any human creature." See *Screenplay,* p. 147, n. to p. 112.

10. Preface to *Back to Methuselah,* 2:xii.

Notes to Part III, Chapter 6
The True Joy in Life

1. "Preface on the Prospects of Christianity" to *Androcles and the Lion*, 5:361.
2. Preface to *Back to Methuselah*, 2:xx.
3. Preface, 2:285.
4. (Boston: Atlantic Little, Brown, 1962).
5. Epistle dedicatory attached to *Man and Superman*, 3:510-11.

Notes to Conclusion
Joan's Last Trial

1. "Animadversiones," pp. 1-4, art. 1-5, in *Aurelianen Beatificationis et Canonizationis Servae Dei Ioannae de Arc Puellae Aurelianensis Nuncupataei; Positio Super Introductione Causae* (Rome: The Vatican Press, 1893); my translation. Hereafter cited as PSIC. Copy in Special Collections Room, Columbia University library, filed under "Catholic Church."
2. "Non ergo Christiana heroica virtus, sed militaris mentes animosque commoverat . . ." "Animadversiones," p. 13, art. 17, in PSIC.
3. "Causa famae hujus non virtutes sed gesta ejus." "Animadversiones, p. 9, art 13. in *Novissima Positio Super Virtutibus* (Rome: The Vatican Press, 1903). Copy in the library of John, Cardinal Wright.
4. "Responsio ad Animadversiones," pp. 40-41, art. 69-70, in PSIC.
5. "Responsio ad Novas Animadversiones," p. 124, art. 165, in *Nova Positio Super Virtutibus* (Rome: The Vatican Press, 1903). The Biblical passage quoted is 1 Cor. 1:22. Copy in Special Collections Room, Columbia University library, filed under "Catholic Church."
6. The defense quoted a passage by Felix Sejourné which contends that "in the light of her natural infirmity, the very success in arms of the Venerable provides more than sufficient proof that her mission was from God, and it has been inferred that she must have been virtuous, since God, it seems, may not confide such undertakings in anyone with whom He is dissatisfied." "Animadversiones," p. 19, art. 28, in *Novissima Positio Super Virtutibus*.
7. "Animadversiones," p. 22, art. 30, in PSIC.
8. "Animadversiones," p. 33, art. 46, in PSIC. The passage quoted is from *Aperçus nouveaux sur l'histoire de Jeanne d'Arc* (Paris: Renouard, 1850), p. 71.
9. "Animadversiones," p. 3, art. 3, in PSIC.
10. "Informatio," p. 74, art. 100, in PSIC.
11. The first of two separately paginated batches of manuscript, p. 179; photocopy in MTP.

12. "Responsio ad Animadversiones," p. 85, art. 145, in PSIC.
13. "Rabelais," in *La Vie littéraire*, 1st. ser., 6:43.
14. "Un Roman et un ordre du jour: Le Cavalier Miserey," in *La Vie littéraire*, 1st. ser., 6:81; first printed in *Temps*, Mar. 6, 1887.
15. WMT 18: 219.

Notes to Appendix
Mark Twain's Bargain with Satan

1. *Mark Twain at Work*, p. 120.
2. The bizarre idea that one may be inoculated against sins by commiting them is developed at length in "Theoretical and Practical Morals," WMT, pp. 191-92 (written 1899), and in "The Morals Lecture" (written 1895-96). See Fred W. Lorch, *The Trouble Begins at Eight: Mark Twain's Lecture Tours* (Ames: Iowa State Univ. Press, 1968), pp. 322-24.
3. Notebook 38, 1905-1908, typescript p. 3, MTP.
4. See the letter to his sister-in-law, Mrs. Orion Clemens, dated June 18, 1858, in *Mark Twain's Letters*, p. 40.
5. *Life on the Mississippi*, chap. 5, he says he had thirty dollars "left" when he departed from Cincinnati, but he does not say what sum it was left from, nor how he came by the money. In my view, this last omission is a particularly suspicious detail.
6. The two pages which Paine devotes to this subject concern Twain's alleged acquaintance with a wholly apocryphal character. MTB, pp. 114-15.
7. The last of Twain's siblings, Pamela Moffett, died in 1904. The story of the bank note appears three times in the autobiographical dictations of 1906 to 1907. See MTA 2:288-89; *The Autobiography of Mark Twain*, p. 348; *Mark Twain in Eruption*, pp. 384-93. The last one amounts to a preliminary sketch for "The Turning Point of My Life."
8. When Twain attempted to read the original draft to Paine and to his daughter Jean Clemens he actually suffered a stroke—the result, in Paine's phrase, of "mental agitation," MTB, p. 1528.
9. *Mark Twain-Howells Letters*, p. 782. Letter dated March 14, 1904.
10. *The Ordeal of Mark Twain*, pp. 24-25.

INDEX

A

Adam: MT on, 22–23, 50, 152; Pierre
Bayle on, 89. *See also* Eden myth
Adams, Henry, 40
Adventures of Huckleberry Finn, The,
51–52, 148
*Adventures of the Black Girl in Her
Search for God, The*, 109, 116, 165n7
Adventures of Tom Sawyer, The, 18,
26, 34
Aestheticism, 72
Aldobrandi, 140
Anderson, Maxwell, 11–12
Androcles and the Lion. See Shaw, Ber-
nard
Anouilh, Jean, 11–12
"Antinaturalism in Extremis." *See*
Dewey, John
Apology for Raymond Sebond. See
Montaigne, Michel de
Apostles, The. See Renan, Ernest
Archbishop: in GBS's *Saint Joan*: 120,
124
Armagnacs, 79
Arthur. *See* King Arthur

B

Back to Methuselah. See Bernard Shaw
Bailey, Sol: in MT's *Which Was It?*
146–47, 148
Barnabas, Franklyn: in GBS's *Back to
Methuselah*, 111
Barrés, Maurice, 71
Bastille Saint Loup, 73
Baudricourt: in AF, 80; in GBS, 100,
101, 108, 115, 117, 118, 119
Bayle, Pierre, 69–70, 72, 89, 163n9
Bentham, Jeremy, 130
Bergeret: in AF's *L'Orme du mail*, 80,
160n19
Bergson, Henri, 106–7, 108–9, 166n12
Berkeley, George, 70
Blake, William, 166n10
Brooks, Van Wyck, 18, 151

Brousson, Jean-Jacques, 64
Browning, Robert, 134
Brustein, Robert, 136–37
Bunyan, John, 99, 109
Burgundy, Duke of, 73
Butler, Samuel, 99, 106, 107, 132, 133,
165n2, 166n9

C

Caesar and Cleopatra. See Shaw, Bernard
Caprara, Augustinus. *See* Devil's advocate
Catherine, Saint. *See* Saint Catherine
Catholic censor (of filmscript *Saint
Joan*): 112, 113, 115, 119, 169n11,
170n9
Catholic doctrine: on original sin,
16–17; on God, 78, 90, 115, 116,
140–41, 143, 168n10; on the supernatural, 78, 115, 116, 168n10; on
the problem of evil, 89–90; on martyrdom, 91–92, 143, on the criteria
for sainthood, 91, 114–17 passim,
125, 139–43 passim. *See also* Christianity
Catholicism: MT on: 38, 158n3; AF
on, 63, 76, 89–93; GBS on, 102,
112–19, 122–27, 142. *See also* Christianity
Catholic sources (of MT's *Joan of Arc*):
general, 16, 26, 28, 48; Mme de
Chabannes, 28, 35, 38, 158n3; Antoine Ricard, 29, 31; John O'Hagan, 35
Cauchon, Pierre: in MT, 40, 47; in
GBS, 117, 118
"Cavalier Miserey, Le," by AF, 143
Chabannes, Mme de. *See* Catholic
sources
Charcot, J.-M. 69
Charles VII; in MT, 28, 37, 38, 44, 48,
140; Renan on, 65; in AF, 73, 79,
88, 91; Catholic views of, 91, 142;
in GBS, 118